Frederick Gard Fleay

Egyptian Chronology

An Attempt to Conciliate the Ancient Schemes and to Educe a Rational System

Frederick Gard Fleay

Egyptian Chronology
An Attempt to Conciliate the Ancient Schemes and to Educe a Rational System

ISBN/EAN: 9783337236359

Printed in Europe, USA, Canada, Australia, Japan

Cover: Foto ©Thomas Meinert / pixelio.de

More available books at **www.hansebooks.com**

EGYPTIAN
CHRONOLOGY

AN ATTEMPT TO CONCILIATE THE
ANCIENT SCHEMES AND TO EDUCE
A RATIONAL SYSTEM

BY

F. G. FLEAY

" Numbers are the only certain things ; they can be
neither controlled nor perverted"
An Egyptian Princess, G. EBERS

LONDON
DAVID NUTT, 270-271, STRAND
1899

THIS ESSAY IS DEDICATED TO THE

MEMORY OF THE LATE

EDWARD WHITE BENSON, D.D.

LORD ARCHBISHOP OF CANTERBURY

(IN ACCORDANCE WITH THE PERMISSION* GRANTED

BY HIM IN HIS LIFETIME)

BY

F. G. FLEAY, M.A.

IN REMEMBRANCE OF THE DAYS WHEN THEY WERE BOTH

DEALTRY THEOLOGICAL PRIZEMEN

AND

SCHOLARS OF TRINITY COLLEGE, CAMBRIDGE

* *As His Grace never saw any portion of the MS.*
it must not be supposed that the book
in any way represents his
views of the subject
thereof

CONTENTS

PREFACE

THE original intention of the present essay was to
collect the numerical statements of the ancient
authorities and to present them side by side so as to
ascertain if possible the common source from which
schemes differing by hundreds and perhaps thousands
of years in their epochs for Menes had derived their
origin. Should the quest prove futile the labour
would not I thought be altogether in vain. For
although the ancient schemes had been carefully
gathered in expensive works (Lepsius' "Königsbuch"
for example) the reproductions of them in the
histories in common use in England were either
very incomplete or mingled with so much hypothetic
guesswork as to be misleading as to what the
ancients really meant: and moreover the present
fashion of depreciating the ancients and throwing
them aside as either grossly erroneous when genuine,
or else as merely post-christian forgeries, did not
appear the most likely method of getting at the
truth.

The first step towards my own conclusions was

the discovery that no ancient authority reckoned
more than twenty *successive* legitimate dynasties.
Then on arranging the various schemes side by side
I found that there were only minor differences for the
twenty-four later dynasties which offered little difficulty against their reconciliation.   But for the first
six dynasties Manetho and the shorter schemes
proved absolutely irreconcilable : the monumental
data showed conclusively that Manetho was wrong;
but I could not determine which of the others was
right.   The editor of the *Athenæum* kindly per-
mitted me to print in that periodical a trial scheme
based on the Chronicler's which elicited from Professor Petrie a letter pointing out that overlaps
between the fourth, fifth, and sixth dynasties were
historically impossible. As all the ancient short
schemes require such overlaps no *one* of them could
be admitted. It was still possible to restore the full
reckoning (without overlap) from the Chronicle and
the Turin papyrus combined.   I tried this and
found on testing the result by Sed festival dates,
&c., that every condition required was satisfied as
far as my knowledge extended.   I now began to
have hopes of getting at something like the true
dates, and rewrote the whole essay.   While re-
arranging the tables I discovered that all the
schemes were manipulated by their authors so as to
get Sothic periods from their epochs for first kings

down to some important change in the condition of the country (such as the Persian conquests) or else to the monarch regnant when the scheme was made. I also noted the parallelism between the intervals in the human and divine dynasties. This new matter, which confirmed my previous conclusions in every detail, could not be incorporated without rewriting the whole essay a third time.

The result of this continual remodelling a treatise, begun in 1892 with a transliteration somewhat like that of Brugsch, greatly altered in 1895 with that of Petrie (which I greatly prefer), and rewritten in 1898–9, has necessarily been a frequent variation in spelling: Sheshonk and Shashank, Merenptah and Mineptah, and the like, occurring sometimes even on the same page. I have been loth to change these because they often indicate the authors from whom I derived the statements in which they occur, but I have been careful when there was the slightest doubt as to the identity of any personage not to name him by a simple numeral but to give both personal and throne names: for instance I do not mention kings of dynasties xi. and xx. simply as Antaf v. or Ramessu xii.

The convenient printing of the tables on separate sheets is due entirely to the liberality of the publisher: I have no claim whatever to any credit for it.

The present instalment is a portion of a larger

work embracing the chronology of the Babylonians, Assyrians, Hebrews, &c., the appearance of which will depend on the sale of the present portion. Directly on the recoupment of the expense of its production the whole will be made ready for the press.

I have to acknowledge the courtesy with which inquiries as to special points have been answered by Prof. F. Petrie, Prof. Sayce, Prof. Rhys Davids, Bishop Barry, Dr. E. A. Abbott, and Prof. Max Müller.

I desire most emphatically to disclaim the opinion formed by one or two friends who have seen the proof sheets that I wish to lower the epoch of human civilisation : positive numbers compel me to adopt a lower epoch than that now in fashion for the introduction of recorded history, which I cannot trace even in monarchic lists to an earlier date than 2924 B.C., but a civilisation which could produce such work as the early sculpture of Egypt before 2500 B.C. must have required many centuries to develop.

F. G. FLEAY.

27 DAFFORNE ROAD, TOOTING, S.W.
July 1899.

EGYPTIAN CHRONOLOGY

INTRODUCTORY

" ALTHOUGH the questions of the Egyptian chronology are among the most difficult, they are also among the most essential to be considered. The various data that exist need that full discussion in the light of modern knowledge of the subject which they have never yet had." These words are Flinders Petrie's : they are weighty and they are true. From Wilkinson to Mariette dates have been attributed to Menes varying from 2429 B.C. to 5735 B.C., assigning a duration of two millenniums at the lowest or more than five millenniums at the highest to this ancient empire, each scheme differing from every other, and satisfactory only to its author. At the present time the long chronology, which places Menes at somewhere about 5000 B.C., is fashionable ; fifty years ago the short system was in vogue, yet no discovery of the last half-century has been of such a nature as to require so radical a change of opinion. The one datum at the root of the sudden veering of chronological ideas (the date assigned to Sargon) will be

A

considered in its due place; for the moment I confine myself to Egyptian data only, and I begin with an attempt to ascertain what were the opinions of ancient native chronologers—a matter universally neglected and even derided by great living authorities, who, while basing their whole systems on an end-to-end elaboration of Manetho's numbers, openly declare that he is absolutely untrustworthy, and that any use of his scheme has had its day. The rules that will guide me in this attempt are the following :

(1) To throw aside no datum, however absurd it may seem, as useless. If it be erroneous, the datum itself may be valueless and yet the mode of the introduction of the error may be of great importance.

(2) To reject no definite statement until it has been shown to be in direct contradiction with a higher authority.

(3) As far as I can to eliminate my own personal equation. I know my tendency to prefer a high antiquity for Egypt, and have repeatedly searched my results after completing my investigation for every instance where this tendency could be traced, and given it careful reconsideration.

Turning then to the ancient Egyptian schemes which are in this essay, I believe, for the first time displayed (in Table I. at the end) synchronistically, we see that only two of these extend through the whole range of the empire from Menes to Artaxerxes Okhos. The first of them, that of the old Egyptian chronicler preserved by Synkellos, gives to this series of dynasties a period of 2324 years, as shown by the totals hereafter given in detail; in the items there is a deficiency of 178 years, which must be inserted somewhere. A comparison with Manetho and with certainly known history (the results of which I am compelled here to anticipate, but they are indisputable) show that the omissions are Dynasty xxi., 128 years, which is altogether dropped, and 50 years in Dynasty xviii., which brings xviii.+xix (244+228 years) into exact accordance with Manetho's xviii.+xix (263+209 years); these insertions are indicated by square brackets in the table, and so are all variations from traditional numbers throughout this essay. It will be noticed that the Chronicler admits only 20 dynasties, including Dynasty xxi. here inserted; for the two following of 6 Tanites and 3 Tanites make only one in the usual nomenclature. The corrected version would read:

xxi.	7 Tanites,	128 years	for	xxi.	6 Tanites, 121 years,
xxii.	9 Bubastites,	169 years		xxii. 3	„ 48 years;

but I shall have to recur to this.

Of the Manethonic schemes there can be no doubt which one is most useful for the present purpose; it is that of the sums stated at the end of each dynasty by Africanus, and the totals of Manetho's three volumes. It is not necessary now to examine the question whether these numbers represent Manetho's own views correctly, as my present object is to explain the grand total of 3555 years expressly stated by Synkellos to be the complete sum of Manetho's dynasties. An examination of Table I.

will show the reader that it is impossible to evolve
this number from either scheme of items as handed
down from Africanus or Eusebius, nor can it be got
from Eusebius' sums. If, however, we take the
stated sums and totals of Africanus, and separate
the dynasties for which the years are given for each
king from those for which the dynastic sums only
are given, arranging them in separate columns, we
get the following result :

	Totals stated		With items		Sums only
Demigods. . . .	214	=	214		
Vol. i. . . .	2300	=	1510	+	{ 783
Omitted . . .					{ [7]
Vol. ii. . . .	2121 }	=	916	+	1306
Omitted . . .	[101] }				
Vol. iii. . . .	1050	=	{ 724 }	+	135
Omitted . . .			{ [191] }		
Grand total .	5784	=	3555	+	2231

There is a discrepancy in each column.   In vol. i.
the sums of the dynasties are 7 years in excess
of the years assigned to the component dynasties ;
and in vol. ii. there is an error of addition of 101
years ; these do not concern us here, and will be
considered by-and-by, but the difference of 191 years
in vol. iii. must be explained, for it falls on the
column which is the subject of the present argument.   If the total at the end of Manetho's third
volume is correctly stated, then the total of the years
from Horus to Okhos is in this reckoning 3555, and
the kings in this column (*i.c.*, those whose years are
individually given in Manetho) are the only legitimate ones, the dynasties without kings' names being

contemporary and subordinate; but if the items are complete, and no satisfactory explanation can be presented for the missing 191 years, then this explanation of the total of 3555 years must be abandoned, and one of the main foundations of my ultimate result be destroyed.

For 48 years of the missing 191 there is no difficulty. The 48 years of the Chronicler's 3 Tanites (Dyn. xxii.) are entirely missing in our versions of Manetho. That they must have been originally inserted in his scheme (that is to say, that his Dyn. xxii. must have been 168 years, not 120) is certain. From Dyn. xxi. to xxx. neither the Chronicler nor Manetho are in error for more than three or four years, if the insertions of 48 years in the latter and 128 in the former are made as required by the totals in each scheme; and that Manetho should have made such an error is not credible to any one who has examined the results of modern research on this period. It will be abundantly proved as we go on that back as far as 1580 B.C. both Manetho and the Chronicler are accurate.

But we have still 143 years to account for, and also to explain how it got into a reckoning at all which is otherwise trustworthy. Help comes here from an unexpected source: Africanus expressly states that the Exodus took place at the beginning of Dyn. xviii. in the year 1797 B.C., and Synkellos tells us that Africanus reckoned the epoch of Okhos at about fifteen or sixteen years before Alexander's coming into Egypt in 332 B.C.—*i.e.*, at 347 or 348. From the Exodus therefore to Okhos was reckoned by Africanus at 1450 years or a year or two less. It will be seen from Table I. that the years actually given in Africanus' reckoning (items) from Dyn. xviii. to xxx. are 1305, which shows a deficiency of 143–5 years. He therefore (or some manipulator of his scheme after him) omitted 143 years at least from his original reckoning, which was taken from some version of Manetho, evidently from the version of sums and totals which we are now considering, in which this 143 years must have originally appeared.

Still further: in the Sothis book (reckoning of Synkellos) there is a dynasty unrecognised elsewhere,

59. Athothis	. . . . .	28 years
60. Kenkenes	. . . . .	39 „
61. Ouennefes	. . . . .	42 „
62. Sousakeim	. . . . .	34 „
Sum	. . . .	143 „

made up of 4 reigns stolen from Dyn. i. 2, 3, 4, and xxi. 7, which contains exactly the years required, and is inserted in the middle of Dyn. xx. I have no doubt that this is the same dynasty as that which must have been included in the version of Manetho which we are now considering, and also in that of Africanus. It follows that the sums version of 3555 years is now fully accounted for, and that this scheme, as well as the Chronicler's, omitted 10 of the 30 dynasties included in the end-to-end reckoning as contemporary and subordinate. There is, indeed, no total or any other indication in any ancient scheme that necessitates more

than 20 successive dynasties; and there is direct evidence that the extreme short and long schemes (chronicle and Manetho-total) of old times each omitted 10 dynasties as subordinate, though not the same 10.

I will next examine each dynasty of the 30, in order to ascertain whether the monuments confirm these ancient authorities in their arrangement; and at the same time, as far as may be, to find out what the true duration of each dynasty was; in other words, whether the long or short chronology of the ancients is more worthy of credit.

SECTION I.

THE DYNASTIES.

MANETHO'S FIRST VOLUME.

DYN. I.–VI.—(*See Table facing this page.*)

THE first important preliminary in this period is to determine whether the Turin total should be read as 755 years (the number given in the papyrus); or 1755 as several high authorities assert, on the hypothesis that the numeral 1 has been destroyed in this very fragmentary document. In support of this view a series of numbers, 73, 72, 83, 95, 95, 70, 74, 70, which occur on another fragment have been assigned to the 9 kings from Mena to Send; these 8 (with

2515	3. Zeserti	[9]	13. 13	17. Teta	5. Soyfis	16
					6. Tosertasis	19
					7. Akhes	42
					8. Sefuris	30
2506	4. [Heni]	[6]		18. Sezes	9. Kerferes	26
	Sum			19. Neferkara	(Kheneres)	

18 years for the 9th king, say) would give us 700 years for this period; and taking the highest numbers possible for the succeeding kings—71 years for the rest of Dyn. ii., 57 for iii., 103 for iv., 191 for v., and 181 for vi.—we should have a total of 1303 years, which is far short of 1755.   Moreover, it is scarcely credible that this papyrus should, in every instance where direct comparison is possible—*e.g.*, in vi. 2–4, v. 7–9, iv. 2–8 (if my arrangement is right), iii. 1–2, ii. 7—have numbers lower than Manetho by 30, 20, 168, 19, and 17 years (254 in all), and in the instance of these 9 kings alone have an excess of 385 years. I shall, later on, give my reasons for supposing that Manetho's object was to add to the true reckoning, in order to obtain a Sothis cycle of 1461 years from Mena to Usertsen i.; while the Turin papyrus, with a like object, diminished the true numbers to get a cycle from Mena to 46 Ramessu i.   It has also been authoritatively stated that 755 years is an impossibly small number for an Egyptian scheme; yet the Chronicler has only 736 years and Eratosthenes 676.   It is to show that 755 is a possible number that I have inserted conjectural years for i., ii. in the Turin column, which differ from Manetho's only in one instance—36 years for Mena (Eusebius has 30).   A further deduction of 26 years would give exact coincidence of 351 years for i. and ii. with Eratosthenes and 443 for i.–iv. 2 with the Chronicler as well.   These two numbers are probably historically wrong, but they refute the statement of "impossibility."

Another important point is my omission of v. 1–6

from the Turin reckoning altogether. Even if they had to be included the 755 years need not be given up; we should only have to diminish the reckoning of i. 1–ii. 3 by an equivalent amount. But in fact there is no other instance in this papyrus of an absolute loss of a group of 6 kings, without indication either of names or numbers, or at least position, in the columns of preceding or succeeding kings. Attempts have been made to assign fragments to this vacancy, especially the fragment which I have placed in iv.; but the exact agreement of the numbers with Eratosthenes on the one hand for the sum, and with Manetho on the other for the smaller numbers, leaves little doubt of its true position. The difference from Manetho lies in the three successive reigns of Kheops, &c., 63, 66, 63 years respectively, which cannot be historical whether Khafra was son or brother of Khufu. These numbers are not so improbable as the 9 reigns of over 70 years each already noted, but these latter no doubt belong to a dynasty of gods. In the present case the proof is definite. Raskhemka was attached to 5 kings—Khafra, Menkaura, Shepseskaf, Userkaf, Sahura. On the Manethonian hypothesis this involves $x+63+7+28+y$ years, a century at the very least, and even with the true number 32 for Menkaura, Raskhemka must have served 70 years and lived for some 90 years—an extreme case. That these large numbers were priestly inventions is also evident from the fact that in the time of Herodotus, although, as we shall see hereafter, they had already been introduced, there was a concurrent tradition assigning 50 years to Kheops and 56 to Khefren : the amount of alteration had not been definitely settled. As to the antecedent probability of such an omission in the Turin papyrus as v. 1–6, 125 years, I think it is more likely than not. If, as I hope it is by this time evident, this reckoning is a short one, and if, as I hope to show when I consider the schemes, which cannot be till I have gone through the details of the dynasties, all the short schemes had the aim of reducing the time from Mena to the reigning monarch to a cycle, similar omissions are to be expected in every case. Now the Chronicler omits iv. 3–end and vi. 1–5, 9–11, but gives v. in full. Eratosthenes omits v. 5–vi. 5, vi. 9–11, but gives iv. in full (omitting Shepseskaf). So the Turin omits v. 1–6, but gives iv. and vi. in full. Fortunately they supplement each other, and from the 3 we can restore the full reckoning without the overlaps between iv. and v., or v. and vi., which they introduced.

And that, at any rate as far back as the beginning of Dyn. iii., we thus get a true reckoning will be more evident if we examine the structure of the Manethonic scheme in detail. No less than 6 kings —Tlas, Sesokhris, Tyreis, Mesokhris, Soyfis, and Akhes—are absolutely unknown on any monument or in any early scheme ; and 3 others—Athothis, Semempses, and Boethos—are found only in the Abydos list, which was, in my opinion, the beginning of corruption on the long system. For compare the following parallels :

i. 2. Athothis	. .	47 years	xii. 1. Sesonkhosis	.	46 years
ii. 1. Boethos	. .	38 „	2. Ammanemes		38 „
8. Sesokhris	. .	48 „	3. Sesostris	. .	48 „
iii. 3. Tyreis	. . .	7 „	4. Lambares	. .	8 „
7. Akhes	. . .	42 „	Successors	.	42 „
Sum	. .	182 „	Sum	.	182 „

and note that Sesokhris was 5 cubits in height and
3 palms in breadth, while Sesostris was 4 cubits,
3 palms, 2 digits in height. Is it possible that two
such prodigies should be found in the same history,
and with nearly the same names, and exactly the
same abnormal reigns? These two are evidently
one; and the exact correspondence of the year
numbers throughout shows that the whole of
Dyn. xii. was re-inserted in i.–iii. to eke out the
extravagant numbers of the Saite calculation, just as
i. 2–4 were used afterwards in concocting the
fictitious Dyn. xxa already noticed. The other
4 kings who were wanted for the 68 years
still deficient were ingenuously inserted with an
average of 17 years each : Semempses, 18 ;
Tlas, 17 ; Mesokhris, 17 ; Soyfis, 16. All these
must surely be rejected as having no sufficient
evidence that they ever existed. There are also
other indications of uncertainty and alteration in the
order of the kings in this group in ii. and iii. It
is most unlikely that any king in the Turin list
should be omitted in the fuller list of Abydos,
which was made at nearly the same time. The
Abydos list has 4 kings: Teta, Sememptah,
Banetern, and Neterkara, which are certainly not
in the Turin ; but the other three, Uaznes, Sezes,

and Neferkara (19), which have no correspondent
Turin kings in the places they now occupy, are
exactly balanced by Neferkara, Sekerneferka, and
Hezefa in the Turin lists. Moreover, two of these
kings cannot be rightly placed at the end of iii.,
where the order is fixed by the Westcar and Prisse
tales as Zeserti, Nebka, Heni, Sneferu, in accordance
with the Sakkara list (almost the only instance of
any aid being derivable from this list beyond a
general confirmation of that of Abydos). I have,
therefore, indicated the true position of these three
kings in parentheses. Their year numbers, 17, 26,
30, as compared with Manetho's 17, 25, 30 at the
end of ii., confirm this conjecture. In like manner
I identify Manetho's Kheneres with Heni [Ra], and
transfer him to the end of iii. If it be objected that
Uaznes and Neferkara cannot be identical, as they
both occur in the Sakkara list, I reply that this
blundering compilation was manifestly made after,
and probably from, the Abydos and Turin lists, and
that it took Uaznes from one, and Neferkara from
the other : it has scarcely any independent authority.
Any difference of names can be paralleled in the
Neterbau for Bezau, and Beby for Zaza in the
Sakkara list.

A very important question is that of the differences of the actual and stated totals in Africanus.
In i. Lepsius was certainly right in maintaining that
the original number for Athothis was 47 years. I
shall by-and-by give my reason for supposing that
the alteration is due to Africanus himself. Eratosthenes had already made a still greater change to

59. In iv. the original number for Bikheris was no doubt 12, not 22, and this change also was, I believe, made by Africanus. But we have for this Dynasty a various reading arising from a series of partial totals inserted in Synkellos, which are certainly not from the same hand as the sums and totals which I have as yet considered. This reckoning is :

Dyn.		Sums
i. 253 years	. . . . .	—
ii. 302 „	. . . . . .	555
iii. 214 „	. . . . . .	769
iv. 277 „	. . . . . .	1046
v. 248 „	. . . . . .	1294
vi. 203 „	. . . . . .	1497
vii. 70 days	. . . . . .	—
viii. 142 years	. . . . .	1639 years, 70 days.

The last column contains the figures actually stated, the others are derived from these by subtraction. As all the other numbers are taken from the sums, not from the items, of Africanus, there must have been a various reading of 277 for 274 in this dynasty, and consequently one of the items has been decreased by 3. It is hard to say which one, but as Khufu has a longer reign than Khafra in each of the short reckonings, I think we should read 66 for 63 for his reign ; anyhow, 277 is almost certainly the original reading. In v. the 30-years surplus in the sum was surely an arbitrary addition by the compiler of the 3555-years total ; there is no reign to which we can add 30 years with any probability, and the agreement of the sum of 191 years (taking the last three reigns from the Turin papyrus) with the Chronicler's 190 forbids any alteration being made.

I may as well anticipate after results at this point by stating that the compiler was certainly not Manetho himself, but the editor of his scheme, not very long after his death. I will call this editor henceforward the Redactor for clearness' sake.

In vi. this Redactor introduced a reign of 100 years instead of a lifetime; the reign was 94 years, as Neferkara Pepy was 6 years old at his accession.

I now pass to the totals from i. 1 to iv. 2. Eratosthenes has 15 kings and 443 years, the Chronicler has 15 generations, 443 years. These statements are manifestly identical, and the notion that the Chronicler meant 15 dynasties is absurd. It was, I think, a guess made by Eusebius; as he has absurdly introduced the numbers 190, 103, 348, 194, which follow in the Chronicler, for his dynasties xvi., xvii., xviii., xix., contrary to all other historical authority. He was probably misled by the notion that the Chronicler must have had 30 consecutive dynasties, whereas really he has but 20 in all, and I cannot find, as I have already stated, any evidence that the ancients ever reckoned any more than these consecutively. In order to get these numbers in, Eusebius had to change " 8 Tanites " (palpably the Elefantine dynasty of Manetho) into " 5 Thebans "; " 4 Memphites " (evidently the last 4 kings of vi., Neterkara being reckoned) into a " Shepherd " dynasty of 4 kings; and " 14 Memphites " into " 14 Diospolites," and then he could not make up his 348 years without including two more

Diospolites (not now extant) in his text.   His whole system is clearly vitiated by personal equation and untrustworthy, in fact scarce worth tabulating, and yet in the very latest modern system some of his most absurd numbers still figure conspicuously. Truly has Petrie said that the chronology of Egypt has never been adequately investigated.

Returning to the Chronicler, he states that these 15 generations were of a " Cynic cycle," *i.e.*, taken from some scheme which had a Sothic cycle for its basis.   I shall show in a subsequent section that there were two such schemes in existence in the Chronicler's time : one of a long chronology (Saite), which cannot be the one he alludes to; the other that of the Turin papyrus.   Now the Turin scheme has 18 kings for this period (average reign 25 years) ; this agrees perfectly with the Chronicler's 15 generations (average 30 years) ; but Eratosthenes, who clearly worked from Manetho's list, mistook the statement, and in order to get his 443 years out of 15 *reigns*, used the long reigns of Mena, Athothis, &c., as given by Manetho, sometimes introducing kings not in the Turin papyrus (the Cynic cycle) at all.   Hence we must not look to Eratosthenes for item numbers in this period ; but his (and the Chronicler's) total of 443 years is most valuable, for the evidence that the Turin list had the same totals, considering the exact agreement thereby produced with its 755 years to the end of vi., manifestly preponderates.

This total (subtracting 14 years for Nitaqerti's successors) gives 741 years from Mena to the end of that queen's reign. The Chronicler has 736 years (nearly the same amount), and Eratosthenes 676 (two Sed periods less). These differences do not need consideration just now, but I must state here that the Manethonic original total (not the Redactor's) of 1461 years, one Sothic period, clearly points to the first motive for his enormous exaggerations, just as the mention of the Cynic cycle by the Chronicler indicates the origin of the under-estimate of the ancient short chronology. In the B.C. dates of the Table I have used the Turin numbers *plus* the 125 years omitted in the papyrus, and have filled in the missing items from the corresponding kings in i., ii. from Manetho, thus introducing 26 more years. The maximum date for Mena would be 2956 B.C., the minimum 2904. For the justification of my mean date (2929) see hereafter under the head of Conclusions, where the existence of an earlier form of the Turin reckoning is deduced.

From this point onward the Manethonic reckoning (corruptions being removed) is substantially accurate, all the intentional falsifications by introducing fictitious kings and exaggerated numbers to the glorification of Memphis being confined to i.-vi. by the Saite or Memphite priests. The corresponding depreciation of the Memphite reigns in the short chronology is due to the Heliopolite priests (Chronicle) or the Thebans (Turin). Eratosthenes the Greek followed the Theban scheme.

There is a palpable objection to my arrangement of the fragment of the Turin papyrus in Dyn. iv. The only name remaining is that of Akauhor, which

should appear as Menkaura. Hence the confidence
with which the fragment has been assigned to Dyn. v.,
where it is assumed that Akauhor, whose name occurs
in three farm-lists of this time, is either the personal
name of Neferfra or else an independent king, otherwise unknown, between Shepseskara and Userenra.
But these are merely guesses. I have met with no
proof that this Akauhor may not be identical with
Menkauhor v. 7, and, if this cannot be allowed, it is
certain that no Akauhor occurs in any list of ancient
date except the Turin. It is far more likely that
Akauhor, Menkauhor, Menkaura, are all versions of
one name. That Ra and Hor can be thus interchanged is certain, as the names Radedef and Hor-
dedef occur indifferently for the son of Khufu (cf. the
Westcar papyrus) and for the son of Menkaura (cf.
the Book of the Dead). It is the latter who is the
king in Dyn. iv. The priests of Dyn. xxvi. confused
him with the former, and placed him after Khafra;
the Abydos list by a similar confusion puts him
next before Khafra. Another instance of names of
different form but identical in substance is to be
found in the Shepseskaf of Dyn. iv. (in Abydos), and
the Shepseskara of Dyn. v. (Sakkara). [Compare
Userkaf v. 1 (Abydos) and Userkheres (Manetho),
which implies the form Userkara.] His misplacement in the Sakkara table arose from the overlap
between iv. and v. introduced in the short chronology. The omission of the last 58 years in iv. by
the Chronicler, or of the first 62 years of v. by
Eratosthenes would equally bring him to the fourth
place in Dyn. vi. I cannot identify him with Suhtes,

B

who reigned probably only a few months, but Aty
may be the same as Suhtes; his pyramid was to
have been called Bau, and pyramid names with Ba
are found only in Dyn. v. He is not known outside
the Hammamat inscription of his first year recording
the fetching of stone for his pyramid.

It follows that Sisires being relegated to Dyn. iv.
we have for v. 8 kings and, adopting the Turin
numbers for the last three of these, 191 years. The
dynasty is called Elefantine (Query of Sakhebu=
Heliopolite); but was surely of Lower Egypt. It is
hardly possible that the Chronicler by his 8 Tanite
kings with 190 years should have meant any dynasty
but this, yet the unfortunate identification of his
dynasty with xvi. by Eusebius and his consequent
substitution of these numbers for the 32 Shepherds
and 518 years of Manetho has vitiated almost every
modern scheme of any importance, and has even led to
the Chronicler being denounced as a post-Christian
forger! Note especially that the succeeding dynasty
in the chronicle is Memphite, which entirely precludes
its transference to the Eusebian position.

Among matters confirmatory of my arrangement,
but needing no detail here, because no one, I suppose,
will dispute them, are the Heliopolite origin of Dyn. v.
and the consequent predominance of Ra worship:
also the assignment of 3 generations to the time from
Khufu through Khafra and Menkaura to Userkaf in
the Westcar papyrus tale which excludes Bikheris,
Thamfthis and Rathoises (except as contemporary
kings); "Thy son shall reign, and thy son's son, and
then one of them" (i.e., one of v. 1–3) are the exact

words : but I must say a word or two on the quarry-
ing of alabaster at Hatnub by Una under Merenra
because so much stress has sometimes been laid on
it. The whole thing is chronologically valueless ;
not only might the difficulty of landing occur within
much wider limits than those which have been
assigned, but our ignorance of the kind of year in
use before the addition of the 5 epacts introduces an
entirely unknown condition into the problem. I
may add that neglecting this factor the date for
Una's arrival at Memphis comes out at November 21,
which would be entirely satisfactory. It is not
because the result would oppose my conclusions that
I leave out this matter altogether as a datum.

I must not, however, omit a warning to the reader
as to the uncertainty of some of the item-numbers :
for instance, in i. where some read 25 years for Zefa
in the Turin papyrus, others read 17 ; for Userkara
in iv. where some read 6 years, others read 6 months
21 days, and others see nothing at all : for Merenra
some read 4 years, others 14. But the main conclusions for this list do not depend on the items : they
depend on the 755 years total, with which the true
items must be consistent ; on the 181 sum for vi. ;
and in a less degree on the 443 total for i.–iv. 2. If
I have been mistaken in filling in item numbers, the
main thesis remains unaffected. And in regard to
the few conjectural numbers inserted I may point
out that nearly all textual errors—*i.e.*, corruptions
that have not been intentionally introduced—have
arisen from two causes : (1) the accidental destruc-
tion of a portion of the numerals either at the begin-

ning or the end of a number ; (2) the misreading of
∩ which means 10, for ‖ which means 2, or conversely. This latter may arise from indistinct writing
or from accidental obliteration of the upper part of
the ∩. Whenever a discrepancy of a multiple of 8
occurs this solution is generally to be looked for.
Thus for Heni in iii. I read 6 years, ‖‖‖ where
Manetho's Kheneres has 30, ∩∩∩ : and then 9 for
Zeserti, because that gives a sum of 53 for iii. as
Eratosthenes has it, and he is the only available
non-Manethonic authority in this place. So I read
12 for Sneferu in iv. because I thus get a sum of 97
for iv. 1–8, the same as Eratosthenes. There may
be an error of a year or two in any of these insertions
—there are very few of them, all enclosed in square
brackets—but if so there must be a compensating
opposite error somewhere else. I take my stand on
the sums and totals.

All questions concerning Sed festivals will be dealt
with in a separate chapter after the survey of the
Dynasties has been completed. The text of Eusebius'
version of Manetho requires some notice at this point.

As this text stands in the Armeno-Latin version
we have :

> 4ta dynastia Memphitorum regum xvii. . . .
> Quique regnarunt annis 448
> 5ta dynastia regum xxxi. Elephantiniorum . . .
> Quorum primus Othius . . . Quartus Phiops . . . usque ad
> annum [100].
> 6ta dynastia
> Mulier quædam Nitocris, &c.

This is palpably corrupt : the 17 kings comprise
Dynasties iv. and v. ; the 448 and the 100 of Phiops

make up 548, just the number needed to bring Eusebius into agreement with Africanus (if for Dyn. iv. we adopt the reading 277 not 274 in the sum): Phiops is therefore reckoned twice : xxxi. cannot be explained ; Othius and Phiops belong to the sixth dynasty. Read therefore :

> 4ta dynastia Memphitorum . . .
> 5ta dynastia Elephantiniorum regum xvii.
> Quique regnarunt annis [5]48
> 6ta dynastia [Memphitorum regum vi.]
>   Quorum primus Othius . . .
>   Quartus Phiops . . .
>   [6ta] Mulier quædam Nitocris . . .

Some scribe has confused the repeated " 6ta " and thus misplaced the " 6ta dynastia"; this led to the misplacing of Phiops and his 100 years in Dynasty v., and this again to the reduction of the 548 to 448. The corruption is certainly due to copyists, not to Eusebius, and all that has been said about his splitting the sixth dynasty and mangling its predecessors may be thrown aside. Eusebius could not have made a dynasty of one queen: as his sum "203 years" amply proves.

It will be shown under the head of Schemes that from this point, 2024 B.C., the Manethonic reckoning is virtually accurate, and that (excepting one omission in Dyn. vii.–x.) that of the chronicle is equally true. For the preceding time Manetho errs grossly in excess. The true reckoning must be evolved from the numbers of the Turin papyrus and the Chronicle (for Dyn. v.) as set forth in my final Conclusions.

DYNASTIES VII., VIII. (MEMPHITE): IX. X. (HERA-
KLEOPOLITE)

It is difficult at this point to decide on the order
of treatment to be adopted; if I take Manetho's
order (as I have done), we must leave xi., which was
contemporary with i.–vi., for future consideration: if
I treat of xi., I must break the continuity between
vi. and vii. I can only choose the less of the two
evils, and ask the reader to suspend his judgment till
we (that is, as always in my way of writing, the
reader and I) reach Dyn. xviii. For this group we
have no items in Manetho, the dynasties not being
considered by the long school as legitimate; but for
the short school they were the only ones reckoned.
The Chronicler, the Abydos list and Eratosthenes
notice no other, and even the Turin, which gives xii.
in full, does so only because, as in the parallel cases
of xi.–xvii., its plan was to include all dynasties
legitimate or other. The notion that it meant all
these to be calculated end to end is purely modern
and quite incompatible with the ancient central
hypothesis, that all chronology must be based on the
epoch of Menes being the beginning of a period of
one or more Sothic cycles which ended in the times
of the several authors of the schemes; as is shown
by definite numbers in the instances where their
statements of totals have come down to us. In the
present instance I will consider the evidence in the
case of each scheme separately. The chronicle gives
us 14 Memphites, 348 years, between dynasties
which are certainly vi. (4 Memphites 103 years;
identical with the 3 kings 107 years of Eratosthenes,

Neterkara being included and Pepy ii. reckoned as
94 years) and xviii. his first Diospolite dynasty.
This 348 years in the chronicle reckoning includes
the whole time from the death of Nitokris to the
accession of Aahmes.   Eratosthenes has against this
16 kings and 369 years with a variant reading of
400 years : and the Turin papyrus the same years
369, but 22 kings : of these, 5 are grouped under
the one king Myrtaios, so that these two schemes
are practically identical.   Manetho has, according to
Africanus, 135 kings, which is absurd ; but his years
are easily reducible to a true reckoning.   For 409
years in Dyn. ix. we must read 109, just as in
Eusebius xiv. we are compelled to adopt 184 and
not 484.   The 300 years thus omitted are wanted
in xi. and thither I would transfer them : so the
total remains unaltered.   Also a missing 4 or 7 years
required by the total of Manetho's vol. i. (according
as we adopt 287 or 284 for the sum of iv.) must be
inserted somewhere in this group ; it is impossible
to place it anywhere in i.–vi. : I put it for vii. and
reject the 70 kings of 1 day each as a late fabrication.
Thus we get the following scheme :

DYN.	EUS.		AFR.		COR.		TUR.		ERAT.		CHRO.	
	K.	Y.	K.	Y.	K.	Y.	K.	Y.	K.	Y.	K.	Y.
A : emhat i. .	1	16	1 16		4	14	4	14	1	22	14	348
vii. . .	5	75	70 0,70d.			4						
viii. . .	5	100	27 146		8	146	18	355	8	144		
ix. . .	4	100	19 409		12	109			1	23		
x. . .	19	185	19 185		7	185			6	180		
Sum .	34	476	136 756		31	458	22	369	16	369	14	348

The numbers in Eusebius are clearly guesses and of no help to us. The king numbers in the "corrected" column are simply my own conjectures to show how the $19 = 7 + 12$ and the $27 = 7 + 12 + 8$ of Africanus may have been obtained: they will not be used in the argument, but the exact agreement between Turin and Eratosthenes in total shows that their schemes were practically identical; while that between the totals in the corrected Manetho to the end of viii. and for the first 9 kings of Eratosthenes, 166 years, indicates the position of Akhthoes ix. 1. Again, the near coincidence of Eratosthenes' sum for his last 6 kings, 180 years (or 185 if the variant reading for No. 36 be adopted), with the 185 years of the Manethonic Dyn. x. proclaims the beginning of this dynasty, and shows that the omissions in the short schemes were made after the reign of Akhthoes. This is the only possible position for him, and indicates that the time omitted was included, or nearly so, in the sovereignty of the hated Hyksos, to avoid any mention of whom was apparently the motive for treating legitimate descent at all through these obscure Memphite kings.

DYN. VII.-X.—(*See Table facing this page.*)

In the table as I have arranged it there is agreement between the Turin and Abydos lists for vi., 8, 11; viii. 2, 6; ix. 2; x. 2; and the four names in ra at the end; and no disagreement whatever; the Khety or Neby names viii. 3, 4, do not exclude the corresponding Hormeren and Sneferka. The Eratosthenes list confirms Petrie's identifications of

DYNASTIES VII. VIII. (MEMPHITE); IX. X. (HERAKLEOPOLITE.)

TURIN.	Y.	ABYDOS.	ERATOSTHENES.	Y.	MON.	B.C.
vi. 8. Neferka	2	42. Neferkara	23. Myrtaios	22	N.	2038
9. Nefers	4					2036
10. Ab.	2	43. Neferkara Neby				2032
11. —y	6	44. Dadkashemara				2030
viii. 1. Lost	[8]	45. Neferkara	24. Thyosimares	12	N.	2024
2. Neferkara	[12]	46. Hormeren				
3. Kheti		47. Sneferka	25. Thinillos	8		2004
4. —y		48. Raenka	26. Semfroukrates	18		1996
5. Lost		49. N. Tererel	27. Khuther	7	R.	1978
6. Neferkara			28. Meures	12		1971
7. Khety			29. Khoimaiftha	11		1959
8. S [khaura]			30. Soikynios	60	S.	1948
9. Lost			31. Peteathyres	16	(42)	1888
			Sum . .	166		
ix. 1. [Ahmeryra Khety		50. Horneferka	32. Stammenemes	23	A.	1872
2. ? Hor						
3. H	89	51. N. Pepysenb	33. Sistosikhermes	89		1849
[Omitted]		52. Sneferka Annu	34. Maris	55		1760
x. 1. Lost		53. . . . ukaura	35. Sifoas	43		1705
2. S . . . . ra		54. Nefer kaura	36. —	5		1662
3. . . . . ra		55. Horkaura	37. Frouron			1657
4. . . . . ra		56. Neferarkarn	38. Amonthantaios	14 (19) 63		1643
5. . . . . ra						
6. . . . . ra			Sum . .	180		
Sum viii–x . .	355					
Total	309		Total . .	369		1580

[To face page 24

Thyosimares and Dadkashemara, Semfroukrates and
Sneferka (not Sneferka Annu however), but not
Meures and Maaabra, nor Thinillos and Tererel.
It makes Khuther, "Tauros tyrannos," equivalent to
Raenka (*ka* the bull, *ra* king), as it should do, and
explains Soikynios as Skhan. Petrie's position for
fragment 48 before 47, *i.e.*, for viii., 1–5 before viii.
6–x. 6, is unquestionably right.

The first king of Dyn. ix. who appears here as
Stammenemes (? Set Amenemhat) is called Akhthoes
by Manetho. Now Akhthoes is certainly a transliteration of Khety, and the missing king in the
Turin list is therefore Abmeryra Khety as Petrie
has it. After Stammenemes there is an omission of
89 years, which singularly enough can be filled
up by the following kings, Kameryra, Maaabra,
Aa, Aahotepra, Neferhepura, and possibly Uazedra
and Yapeqher. The scarabs of these kings, with
those of Neby, Neferkara, and Raenka, form with
one exception all the remains of these dynasties
that have reached us.

But the exception is important. Prince Khety ii.
of Asyut "lived under Kameryra; he built a temple
and prepared a tomb for himself. He also chastised
the Southerners [Thebans], the king himself joining
in the campaign, after which the people of the capital
Herakleopolis came out to meet the king in triumph"
(Petrie).

Now a palette with this king's name was found
(? at Asyut) along with copper open work with the
name of Abmeryra. The two kings must be near in
date, and Kameryra must come after Abmeryra, who

was the first Herakleopolite king. Putting him in the first vacancy as ix. 4, his date will be about 1840 onwards, just after the Hyksos invasion, when the dissensions of the native rulers made the conquest of the country so easy. Thebes at this time had no independent ruler; Dyn. xii. ended in 1840; the Delta was in the hands of the Hyksos, but the invaders did not conquer Thebes till 1731. We have here a clear evidence of contemporary dynasties, but there is no evidence for the arbitrary dictum that these dynasties "must have been" ix. and xi. The statement that "the South *rebelled* from Elefantine to Qau" is dead against it. We know a fair amount of the history of the latter part of Dyn. xi., but it gives no inkling of any subjection to a Herakleopolitan rule.

I have not inserted any of the kings in the gap in the table, because there is nothing to indicate their order. But the amount of the gap itself (89 years) requires some notice. The Turin version as we have it certainly dates from Ramses ii., and I have already pointed out that from its date for Menes, 2690, to 45 Ramses ii. is just a Sothic cycle. Now if there were an earlier version, in which there was no gap, all the kings of Dyn. ix. being duly inserted in it, it would throw back the date of Menes to 2779, and an exact Sothic cycle from 2779 brings us to 1318, the epoch of Ramses i. I think there is great likelihood of this being the true state of the case, and that there was a version containing these kings extant at that time. And so Maspero ("Dawn of Civilisation," i. 233, note, Eng. vers.) says

DYNASTY XI. (DIOSPOLITE.)

MONUMENTS.	Y.	KARNAK.	Y.	SYNKELLOS.	Y.	B.C.
1. [Neferkhara]		1. [Mentuhotep i.]		1. Mestraim	35	2381
2. [Antef i.]		2. Rakhemsmentat		2. Kourodes	63	2281
3. Rasesheshertermaat		3. [Antef ii.]		3. Aristarkos	34	2246
4. Antefaa		4. Antef iii.		[Omitted]	3]	2183
5. Raseshesapmaat		5. Antef iv.		4. Spanios	35	2149
6. Nebhotep	49+	6. Mentuhotep vi.		5.	72	2146
7. Haruahankh		7. Antef v.		6.		2130
8. Nebtauira		8. Mentuhotep iii.				
9. ?		9. Antef vi.		Sum	240	2088
10. Antef vii.	3+	10. Nubkheperra				
11. Mentuhotep iv.	46+	11. Nebkherra				
12. Sankhkara	8+	12. Sankhkara				

Sum in Manetho, 16 kings, 43 years; in Turin, 6 kings, 243 years.

KARNAK LIST.

1. [i. 1. Mestraim]	9. [xi. 3.] [Antef]	17. [xii. 1.] Sehotepabra	24. [xii. 2.] Kheperkaru
2. [iv. 1.] Sneferu	10. [xi. 4.] Antef	18. [xii. 3.] Nubkaura	25. [xvii.] Sanenra
3. [v. 2.] Sahura	11. [xi. 5.] Antef	19. [xii. 4.]	26. [xvii.] Senekhtenra
4. [v. 6.] An	12. [xi. 6.] Mentuhotep	20. [xii. 5.]	27. [xv. 1.] Suserenra
5. [v. 8.] A . . . ses	13. [xi. 7.] Antef	21. [xii. 7.] Maakherura	28. [xi. 10.] Nubkheperra
6. [v. 9.]	14. [xi. 8.] [Mentuhotep]	22. [xii. 8.] Sebeknefrura	29. [xi. 11.] Nebkherra
7. [xi. 1.] Rakhemsmentat	15. [vi. 3.] Pepy	23. [xi. 9.] Antef	30. [xi. 12.] Sankhkara
8. [xi. 2.]	16. [vi. 4.] Merenra		31. [? xviii.]

[To face page 27.

that the papyrus was "written under Ramses i."
We might extend this hypothesis, and suppose a
third still earlier form with Dyn. v. complete, a
lengthened period for Dyn. i., and a date for Menes,
2929 ; the Sothic cycle would then end in 1468
under Tahutmes iii., a likely time for chronological
scheme making, when the Karnak list was made.
Beyond the one incident recorded above nothing
whatever is known of this group; they may have
been subordinate to any dynasties whatever so far as
we know, except for a few years at a time of crisis
when they claimed supremacy over Thebes. If they
occupied the position usually assigned to them, where
are their pyramids ?

DYN. XI.—(*See Tables facing this page.*)

This dynasty is in its earlier portion vague and
uncertain; the Abydos list notes only 2 kings
and the Turin list 6 ; the Karnak list and the
monuments show 9 at least. But the date of the
close of the dynasty is fixed, as Manetho's named
king series makes xii. 2 follow immediately on vi.
He is the only authority who traces the main succession through the Diospolites and Hyksos; Eratosthenes and the Chronicler, as we have seen, following
the Memphites and Herakleopolites.

The 6 kings and 240 years given in the list of
Mestræans by the author of the Sothis book agree so
exactly with the Turin papyrus that I have little
doubt that in this instance (as in others when he
could get no name list from Africanus and Eusebius)

he had recourse to some good authority unknown to us.

I have given the Karnak table in full, as it is the most complete list we have. The lines of the original are for convenience printed as columns to be read downwards : 9–13, 23, 28–30 (9 kings) certainly belong to this dynasty, and I think 7, 8, 14 do so as well ; 8 is certainly not a king of v. or vi. The order appears right.

The first six items in col. 1, 2, 3 (*i.e.*, lines 1, 2, 3 of the original) evidently form in each instance a continuous series ; then come breaks, after which the remaining vacancies were filled up with the overplus of kings still outstanding. Nos. 1–22 form a fairly continuous series, xi. coming between v. and vi., with which two dynasties it was contemporary ; but xii. 2 was omitted in its true place, and put in by afterthought, and xi. 8–12, for whom there was no room in the xi. column, were put in last, but in true order.

There seems to be no room for a seventh king in the Turin list, which contained originally the 6 kings from Nebhotep to the end, but only the 2 last now remain, and these 2 are the only ones noticed in the Abydos list. The sum of 243 years (Turin) compared with the 240 of the Sothis requires 3 years to be inserted somewhere, and I give them to king 9. Perhaps the Turin list made him co-regnant with his father or with Nebtauira, and gave his coadjutors three more years. Anyway he is omitted in the Sothis. There is, however, nothing definite beyond this to oppose the Sothis book, and the long reign of Horuahankh fixes his position as the 2nd in that list. The succession is pretty certain. I have followed the Karnak list in direct order throughout.

It will be noticed that the Sothis makes the first king of this dynasty Mestraim = Menes, with a date of 2724 B.C. according to Synkellos. Really there were several earlier kings than Nebhotep, besides a prince Erpaha Antepa, who ruled over the South under an unnamed king, I think Userkaf v. 1. If so, Nebkhara, whom I venture to insert in the vacancy in the Karnak list—he has hitherto been unplaced but certainly is very early, and all Mentuhoteps have names in Neb—was the first king to rebel; and if this view that xi. was a dynasty that threw off the yoke of the comparatively strong kings of v. be a true one, there may possibly be some confirmatory circumstances recorded in the monuments of v. or vi. Now the reigns of Teta vi. 1, and of Horuahankh xi. 7, were on my reckoning contemporary for 22 years, 2205–2183, and the last connexion of any Memphite king with Abydos that I have been able to trace is the alabaster vase bearing the name of "Teta beloved by Dadet," which was found at that place. But Horuahankh captured the nome of Abydos, and opened its prisons (Stele at Elefantine : Petrie, *Season 1887*). This is a very strong coincidence. The capture took place some time during those 22 years. Again, for 35 years, 2145–2110, Pepy ii. (vi. 5) and Nubkheperra were contemporary. Pepy ii. built in the temple at Koptos, and two sculptured slabs of his are still extant ; but on the doorway

of Usertesen i. a decree of Nubkheperra, third
year (2143 B.C.) has been either built in or copied.
It would appear from this that Nub took Koptos
from Pepy while the building of this temple was in
progress, and continued the work himself. But his
work was afterwards replaced by that of Usertesen i.
who turned many sculptured slabs face downward to
form a pavement. Here again we find no after
mention of Koptos under a Memphite king, and the
evidence from this double coincidence is almost
invincible. Finally there are the inscriptions at
Elefantine by

Pepy ii.	Pepy i.	
	Unas	Horuahankh :

the stele of Dyn. xi. was probably the earliest or at
any rate the second. It is unlikely that Pepy i.
should have crowded in his name and titles above
the stele of Unas had the much better position of
Horuahankh's tablet not been already filled. This,
however, I do not regard as important.

The attempts of modern chronologers to retain and
explain Manetho's 43 years are futile; even the 2
last kings are known to have reigned more than
54 years on monumental evidence, and Manetho
reckoned 16 kings. As 6 kings of these reigned 243
years (Turin) we cannot make the omitted numeral
less than 3 without disturbing the text by unauthorised conjecture, which is quite unnecessary.
The 343 years thus obtained exactly agree with
my reckoning of 109 years for ix. as shown above.

The relative date of the end of xi. is fixed by the

DYNASTY XII. (DIOSPOLITE.)

Abydos.	Mon.	Years.	Turin.	Adopted.	B.C.	Africanus.	Years.	Egs.
59 Sehotepabra	A. i.	29 +	[1]9	19	2053	Ammenemes cotemp. xi.	16	16
60 Kheperkara	Co-reg. U. i. Co-reg.	44 +	45 +	10 / 32	2034 / 2024	1. Sesonkhosis	46	46
61 Nubkaura	A. ii. Co-reg.	34 +	[31]	4 / 28	1992 / 1988	2. Ammanemes	38	38
62 Khakheperra	U. ii.	9 +	[1]9	3 / 19	1960 / 1957	3. Sesostris	48	48
63 Khakaura	U. iii.	26 +	3[8]	38	1938	4. Lakhares	8	8
64 Tmaaenra	A. iii.	44 +	4[7]	47	1900	5. Ammeres	8	
65 Maakherura	A. iv.	6 +	Y. M. D. 9 3 27	9	1853	6. Ammenemes	8	42
Sebeknefrura	Queen.	—	3 10 24	4	1844	7. Skemiofris	4	
Sum .			213 1 17	213	1840	Sum .	160	182
Sum without A. i. .			184	184		Stated .	160	245

[To face page 31.

16 or 14 years which elapsed between Sankhkara and Usertsen i. "After these Ammenemes (Amen-emhat i.) reigned 16 years," are the words quoted by Africanus, but 14 is more likely; from the death of Nitokris. The reign of Amenemhat was 29 years, 13 or 15 of which were spent by him in establishing his position, and founding a new dynasty. He was not a lineal descendant or successor of Sankhkara, but his rival opponent. Dyn. xii. does not therefore succeed xi., but reduces it (for 13 or 15 years) and its successor (Dyn. xiii. as I arrange the dynasties) to a subordinate though still by no means a contemptible or unimportant position.

The race displaced by Dyn. xi. was probably the "new race" discovered by Petrie, who were located about thirty miles north of Thebes. Their date would be contemporaneous with Dyn iv., which agrees with the proved facts that they were later than the earlier reigns of Dyn. iv. and anterior to Dyn. xii. Their contracted burial position, which differs from that of the Medum cemetery, which was still earlier, shows that both Memphites and Thebans alike dispossessed races of an origin quite unlike their own.

THE SECOND VOLUME OF MANETHO.

DYN. XII.—(*See Table facing this page.*)

For this dynasty the Turin list unquestionably gives the true numbers, one of which is unfortunately lost and three are mutilated. The monumental data for co-regencies are :

$$30. \text{ A. i.} = 10. \text{ U. i.}$$
$$41. \text{ U. i.} = 2. \text{ A. ii.}$$
$$35. \text{ A. ii.} = 3. \text{ U. ii.}$$

These monumental years are reckoned from the beginnings of the co-regencies of the Kings; the lists usually reckon from the beginning of their sole reigns (indeed, they could hardly do otherwise without confusion). The mixing up of these methods has caused many errors and unnecessary difficulties in modern schemes, especially in the present instance. I shall have therefore to examine the reign-numbers in detail.

1. Amenemhat i. This king reigned certainly 29 years and some months, 10 of which were shared by Usertesen i. as co-regent. The missing numeral in Turin is probably a 1.

2. Usertsen i. There are dated monuments of this king's sole reign from his 7th year to his 41st. These date from his co-regnancy with his father. The account of his building the temple at Heliopolis is dated in his 3rd year from this epoch. More than 6 months have been lost in the papyrus. As the co-regnancy began in the year 42 it must have lasted 4 years.

3. A. ii. The co-regnancy with U. ii. began in year 32, and the whole reign was therefore $4+28+3 = 35$ years, which just includes the highest monumental data. The number 31 is calculated from the sum, all the other reigns being fixed by other considerations.

4. U. ii. This reign consists of $3+9=12$ years. The highest monumental date is of the 10th year,

but as Manetho states that he took 9 years in conquering Asia, and as the dates have to fit in very tightly if we assign him a reign of 9 years only, I have inserted a conjectural [1] in the Turin list, as high authorities have done before me. Nevertheless, a reign of 9 years only is quite possible, in which case we should have to read [2]9 years for Amen-hotep i. and lengthen the reign of Usertsen i. by 10 years; and this would agree better with the numbers of Manetho. The probabilities in favour of either arrangement are very equally balanced.

5. U. iii. and 6. A. iii. The missing units cannot be far from the 8's of Manetho. I make one a 7 to counterbalance the 9 corresponding to Manetho's 8 in the next reign. A co-regency occurs here between A. iii. and A. iv., but its amount is quite unknown. Turning to Manetho, the years of 4 reigns have evidently been transposed, and for [Kh]akheres I would read 32 years instead of 8 (∩∩∩ıı for ııııııı). Then making the transposi-tion we get 2. Ammenemes, 32; 3. Sesostris, 8; 4. Khakheres, 38; 5. Ammeres, 48; substantially the same as the Turin. Eusebius has nearly the same numbers, but probably read 30 for 32 for Khakheres. The transposition of the numbers was introduced, I think, early; before the time of Dyn. xxvi.; but the corruption of 32 into 8 not till after the time of Josephus. I shall have to recur to this.

The sum 42 years in Eusebius for kings 6–8 indicates a reckoning of 30 years for Ammeres; we get thus 182 for Eusebius' total without Ammenemes, and 198 with him. This 182 was, I feel certain, Manetho's original reading. The true estimate of 184 years was altered when the addition of 24 years to Dyn. xv. (of which more by-and-by) was introduced so as to obtain the sum of these two dynasties unaltered—$160 + 284 = 184 + 260$. The stated sum in Eusebius—245 years—is evidently corrupt, the 45 having crept in from some duplication of Sesonkhosis. Eusebius' sum stated here should read 200 years. In this way, and in no other that I can discover, is the total for the years of Manetho's second volume, 2222, preserved intact; and a careful investigation of Eusebius' numbers shows that in every instance, however violently he may have dislocated specific items, he always carefully preserved the sums whenever any were definitely assigned.

The Mestræan list in Synkellos is worthless in itself, but is noticeable as a good example of the treatment of Manetho's numbers by post-Christian writers. Comparing it with Africanus we find:

DYN.	SOTHIS.	AFRICANUS.
xii. 1	23	16
2	49 } $= 100$	$= \{ 46 \}$ $= 100$
3	29	38
4	—	48
5	2 } $= 15$	$= \{ 8 \}$ $= 16$
6	13	8
7	9 } $= 13$	$= \{ 8 \}$ $= 13$
8	4	4

Sesostris is entirely omitted: the other numbers are disguised by alteration, but the sums are nearly

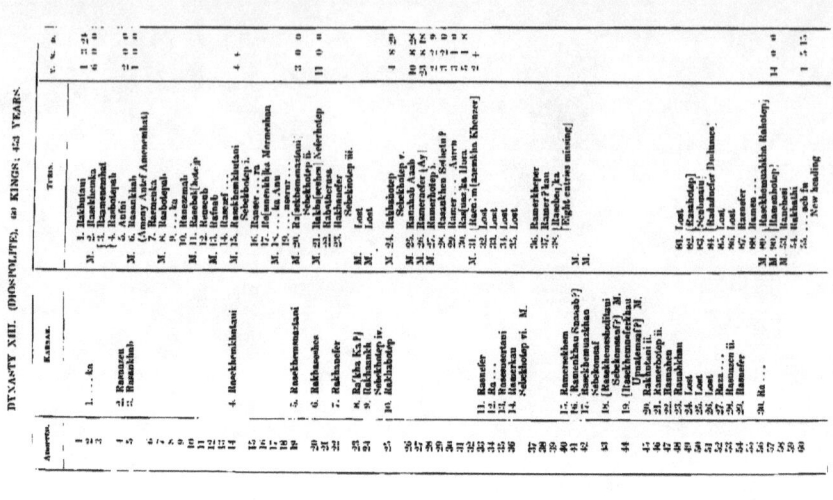

DYNASTY XIII. (DIOSPOLITE.) 60 KINGS. 453 YEARS.

right. I shall in future not notice this scheme from the Book of the Sothis for the dynasties in which Manetho gives the regnal years in detail. For these its author nearly always uses Eusebius' numbers with many alterations of his own.

DYN. XIII.—(*See Table facing this page.*)

As this dynasty does not appear in the Chronicle, and is not reckoned in the 3555 total of Manetho's Redactor, it must be a contemporary dynasty. The only possible place for it is parallel to xii. and its successors. I place it therefore as a direct continuation of xi. We shall on this hypothesis for the period 2024–1580 have 3 lines of succession at least, to say nothing of xiv. and xvi., as follows :

B.C.	MEMPHITE.	LEGITIMATE.	SUBORDI-NATE.	HYKSOS, ETC.	AFRICA-NUS.
2053		Amenemhat i.			
2038	Nitokris dies		xiii. 453		
2033–4		A. i. and U. i.			
2024	vii., viii. 150	xii. Usertsen, 184		xiv. 184	xii. 160
1874	ix. 109				
1840		Hyksos, 109		xv. 260	xv. 284
1765	x. 185				
1731		xvii. 151			
1580	x. ends	xvii. ends		xv. ends	

The sums correspond exactly : vii.–x., 444 years ; xii. 2–xvii., 444 years ; xiv.–xv., 444 years ; all ending at 1580 B.C., when xviii. commenced : xiii. ends 1585 or 1587 B.C., when the final combined struggle against the Hyksos began. But will the items of history— and we have a good many for xiii. and more for xii. —prove to be compatible with the ancient "con-

DYNASTY XIII. (DIOSPOLITE), 60 KINGS; 453 YEARS.

ADOPTED.	KARNAK.	TURIN.	Y.	M.	D.
1	1. . . . ka	M. 1. Rakhutaui	1	3	24
2		M. 2. Rasekhemka	6	0	0
3		{ 3. Raamenemhat			
4	2. Raguazen	{ 4. Rashotepab			
5	3. Rasankhab	5. Aufni	2	0	0
6		M. 6. Rasankhab	1	0	0
		(Ameny Antef Amenemhat)			
7		7. Raemenka			
8		M. 8. Rashotepab			
9		9. . . . ka			
10		M. 10. Ranezemab			
11		M. 11. Rasebek[hote]p			
12		12. Rensenb			
13		M. 13. Rafuab			
14	4. Rasekhemkhutaui	14. Rasezef . . .			
		M. 15. Rasekhemkhutaui Sebekhotep i.			
15		16. Rauser . . . ra			
16		17. Ra[sunenkh]ka Mermeshau			
17					
55	30. Ra . . .	88. Ramen . . .	4	+	
56		M. 89. [Rasekhemuahkha Rahotep]			
57		M. 90. [Raamenhotep]			
58		M. 53. Ranehesi	14	0	0
59		54. Rakhathi			
60		55. . . . neb fu	1	5	15
		New heading			

[To face page 35.

right. I shall in future not notice this scheme from
the Book of the Sothis for the dynasties in which
Manetho gives the regnal years in detail. For these
its author nearly always uses Eusebius' numbers
with many alterations of his own.

DYN. XIII.—(*See Table facing this page.*)

As this dynasty does not appear in the Chronicle,
and is not reckoned in the 3555 total of Manetho's
Redactor, it must be a contemporary dynasty. The
only possible place for it is parallel to xii. and its
successors. I place it therefore as a direct continuation of xi. We shall on this hypothesis for the
period 2024–1580 have 3 lines of succession at least,
to say nothing of xiv. and xvi., as follows :

B.C.	MEMPHITE.	LEGITIMATE.	SUBORDI-NATE.	HYKSOS, ETC.	AFRICA-NUS.
2053		Amenemhat i.			
2038	Nitokris dies		xiii. 453		
2033–4		A. i. and U. i.			
2024	vii., viii. 150	xii. Usertsen, 184		xiv. 184	xii. 160
1874	ix. 109				
1840		Hyksos, 109		xv. 260	xv. 284
1765	x. 185				
1731		xvii. 151			
1580	x. ends	xvii. ends		xv. ends	

The sums correspond exactly : vii.–x., 444 years ;
xii. 2–xvii., 444 years ; xiv.–xv., 444 years ; all ending
at 1580 B.C., when xviii. commenced : xiii. ends 1585
or 1587 B.C., when the final combined struggle against
the Hyksos began. But will the items of history—
and we have a good many for xiii. and more for xii.
—prove to be compatible with the ancient "con-

temporaneous " reckonings of the Chronicle and the Redactor? If they will not bear this severe test, we are driven for xiii. to the end-to-end system of the moderns. Let us examine the particular items one by one as far as space will allow.

Amenemhat i. (probably, as Brugsch supposed, a descendant of the Amenemhat who with 10,000 men fetched stone from Hammamat under Mentuhotep ii.) reigned 29 years, 14 or 16 of which were subsequent to xi. (Africanus); he was, therefore, for 13 or 15 years struggling to establish his supremacy over them. This he succeeded in doing 2038 B.C., when xi. became extinct. At the same time Nitokris died, and vi., which had been greatly weakened by wars with xi. in its last half-century, also became extinct. Amenemhat established vii. and xiii. to succeed vi. and xi. in Memphis and Thebes respectively; but under the suzerainty of xii., which was from this time the central supreme authority. In the later part of his reign Amenemhat left Thebes and established his royal residence at Titoui, a little south of Dahshur. Khutaui, the first viceroy of Thebes, only reigned 1 year 3 months, and his successor 6 years. In 2033 B.C. Usertsen i. was associated in the central rule, and for somewhat over 5 years Rashotepab Amenemhat i. ruled over Thebes, while his coadjutor Usertsen lived at Titoui. This follows from the appearance of his name in the Turin list for xiii. It seems incredible that any king, after an interval of 450 years, should have assumed the full double title of so illustrious a predecessor, and still more so that two successive kings should have divided his names between them, as in the usual modern hypothesis.

In 2024 Raameny Antef acceded at Thebes. I have little doubt that this was the King Arminon in whose reign the 5 Epacts were first used. These days, which were added to the sacred year of 360 days so as to get a nearer approximation to the actual course of the seasons, are first mentioned under Amenemhat i., and on his decease in 2024 were probably established by law. I shall have to recur to this when I treat of the Sed festivals. The names correspond exactly; for that Ar may be a Greek transliteration of Ra is proved by the variants Ar-messes and Ra-messes for Ramessu; Min is known as a contraction of Amen and An of Antef, so that Ar-min-on is a strict equivalent for Ra, ameny, Antef. It is also noticeable that Dyn. xiii. appears at Karnak only under this king, until we come to the time of the Sebekhoteps. So far, then, my hypothesis as to the position of this dynasty agrees with the facts.

The next 8 reigns appear to have been peaceable and to have occupied about 140 years, with an average reign of 17 years, the only known historical fact concerning them being the building of a pyramid at Dahshur by Rafuab. The other brick pyramid at this place was built by Usertesen iii. who, in my reckoning, was Rafuab's contemporary.

But the next king — Rasekhemkhutaui Sebek-hotep i.—gives definite tests for or against my arrangement. In each of his first four years there is a Nile record at Semneh. According to modern hypotheses these records were kept in the reigns of Amenhotep iii., iv.; then abandoned; and revived, for four years only, under Sebekhotep i., some century afterwards at the lowest reckoning; the intervening kings having been utterly careless of establishing any memorial of the maximum rise of the river during this time. So strongly has this difficulty been felt that Rakhutaui xiii. 1 has been identified with Sebekhotep i., and "sekhem" has been interpolated into his name on very slender grounds. In my view Sebekhotep was contemporary with Amenhotep iii., whose Nile records were made in years 5, 7, 9, 14, 15, 22, 23, 24, 30, 32, 37, 40, 41, 43. There is room for Sebekhotep's 4 consecutive years after 9 or 15 or 24 or 32. I think the most probable place is after 15. Later than this he would not be so likely to be acting as a sort of deputy for Amenhotep; he was then probably busy in asserting his own supremacy. I make the date of his 4 years 1884–1 B.C.

Maspero says: " The way in which the monuments of Sebekhotep Sekhemkhutaui and his papyri are intermingled with the monuments of Amenemhat iii. at Semneh and in the Fayum show that it is difficult to separate him from that monarch." Difficult? Is it possible? If it is, should not the possibility be clearly displayed?

Sekhemkhutaui also constructed a large hall in the temple at Bubastis which Usertesen iii. had rebuilt. There are no traces there of Amenemhat iii., in whose reign I suppose the rule over this town to have passed from xii. to xiii. In like manner Tanis, where Usertesen iii. had also built, appears in the possession of xiii. 16 Rasmenka Mermeshau very shortly afterwards, as evidenced by his statues. The six reigns (14–19) seem to have been short (average 4 years), as is usual in times of struggle for supremacy. I date these as about 1884–1858. During this time—in about 1872—Set Amenemhat Abmeryra Khety (Akhthoes) was set up at Herakleopolis. He may have been named after the Diospolite ruler, or he may have been Amenemhat iv. while yet a prince, before his accession in 1853; but the story of his being swallowed by a crocodile (Sebek) seems to me to be an adumbration, either of his exclusion from participation in the pyramid and temple of Hawara at the entrance of the Fayum by his sister Sebeknefru, or of his supersession by Sebekhotep iii. This is, however, mere conjecture. What is certain is that Rakhaseshes Neferhotep [? 1855–1844] is the earliest king of Dyn. xiii. who has left widely spread indications of extensive rule. His residence was north of Abydos, which agrees with the occupation of the Delta by his immediate predecessors already pointed out. He repaired the temple of Abydos, which down to Usertesen iii. was in the possession of Dyn. xii.; he was "beloved of Sebek in the midst of Shed" (Krokodilopolis), which town was occupied by Amenemhat iii. in the early part of his reign at any rate; he was regent at Karnak, which had been forsaken by Dyn. xii. from Usertesen i. onward, and his monuments are found at Shut er Regal, Aswan, Sehel, and Konosso. Everything agrees with the hypothesis that the sceptre had virtually departed from Amenemhat iv. by his fifth year, although he and his sister retained the nominal sovereignty for 9 years more.

Rakhanefer Sebekhotep iii. [? 1844–1840], whether brother or grandson of Neferhotep, whether sole ruler or co-regent, certainly supplements his monuments remarkably. North to South we find him from Bubastis and Tanis through Karnak and Gebelen to Arqo. Those contemporary brothers (as I believe them to be) ruled from one end of Egypt to the other, and therein lay their weakness; the Herakleopolitan was hostile; the twelfth dynasty were retiring on the Fayum and were also hostile; in 1840 the Hyksos swept down and expelled the thirteenth dynasty from Bubastis, Tanis, and the whole of Lower Egypt, but as yet left them Abydos and Thebes, while Herakleopolis and the Fayum, as far as I can trace, never fell under the power of the Hyksos at all. The exact point at which Bubastis and Tanis disappear from the records of Dyn. xiii. is at 23 Rakhaka, whose date would therefore be about 1840 B.C. Between this time and the epoch of Dyn. x. we find 24 Sebekhotep iv. Rakhaankh at Koptos, 26 Rauahab, "beloved of Sebek, lord of Suuaz," and 36 Ramerkau Sebekhotep vi. at Karnak. It would, therefore, be against the thirteenth dynasty, being still in possession of Thebes and Koptos, that the Herakleopolitan Kameryra made his expedition. The internecine civil dissensions continued after the Hyksos had taken the Delta and this accounts for their singular success. Then the Sebekhoteps came to an end, and the Sebekemsafs (42, 43), who head the second series in the Karnak lists, continued the struggle; till in 1731 the Hyksos, under Apepa Raaauser, took Thebes and set up the subordinate dynasty xvii. There is no further record that can be certainly allocated; but the titles of Rahotep, who built at Koptos, are so like those of the early part of xviii. that I place him as 56. His name, Sekhemuahkha, agrees with the ...uah... of the Turin lists. If this be right Ramenhotep, with his 14 years, must come as 57, and the negro Nehesi is fixed by the new heading after 60 as certainly 58. He was in possession of Tanis and Bubastis, and must have lived in the time of the final struggle when the Hyksos were expelled by "the kings of Thebais (xvii.) and the other provinces of Egypt (xiii., x.) in a long and mighty war" (Josephus from Manetho). In 1587 Dyn. xiii. appears to have been absorbed into xvii. The connexion by descent between xviii., which certainly followed xvii. immediately, and xiii. must have been very close, as no less than half of the list of ancestors of Tahutmes iii. at Karnak is assigned to this dynasty.

Such is the position of Dyn. xiii. on my hypothesis. I am not aware of having omitted any known record that has chronological bearing: all the facts appear to fit in, and the positions of Amenemhat i. and Sebekhotep i. seem to give positive evidence in its favour. On the received system the difficulty of making Sebekhotep i. at all near to Amenemhat iii. is to me insuperable.

As regards the list of these kings, it will be seen that I have followed the Karnak list rigidly, and so far from finding its order "wild and hopelessly untrustworthy," I find no reason whatever to doubt its accuracy. In the Turin list I have made one innovation only by introducing the fragment 81–90 (Petrie) which is usually given to xiv. I get this by identifying 87 Rasnefer with 29 Rasnefer in the Karnak list, and the ...uah... of 89 then comes just where Rasekhemuahka is wanted. A few other names are inserted from the monuments in brackets, not with the intention of fixing their position, but merely to show that there is room for them. These names of uncertain place have not been used as data for any argument; but I may mention that 39 ? Sebeqka is "beloved of Sebek, lord of Sunu"; that 49 ? Rasa Hotep occurs at Shut er Regal; 50 ? Senbmaiu at Gebelen; and that 51 ? Radadnefer Dudumes, found also at Gebelen, has a scarab of apparently about the time of Dyn x. (Petrie). But the most striking series of inscriptions is that at Aswan. Nebkherra, Mentuhotep, Amenemhat i., Usertesen i., Amenemhat ii., Usertesen ii., Usertesen iii., Amenemhat iii. all left inscriptions there, but under xiii. there is no notice of this kind until the family tablet of 20 Neferhotep. On my reckoning this would come closely subsequent to Amenemhat iii.; on the popular hypothesis 21 reigns and nearly 2 centuries elapsed during which there is an absolute dearth of any inscriptions whatever. How can this be explained?

ליי

DYNASTY XIV, WITH PETRIE'S NUMERATION

54	Raseheb	76	Raa		113	Lost
55	Ramerzefau	77	Hakha		114	Lost
56	Rasenhka	78	Raankbka	13		
59	Ranebzefaura	79	Rasmen			
60	Ranben	80	Lost		115	Ra.
61	Lost					

38	Lost	91	Lost		125	Anab
40	... mes	92	Lost		126	Ra ... s
41	Ra ... moat....	93	... A		127	Peneus ... n Sept
42	Ranben Hora	94	A		128	Pednuebti
43	... ka	95	A			
44	Raman	96	... ka		47	Ha ...
45	Ra	97	Lost		48	Sa
46	Lost					

62	... zefa			14		
63	... uben	98	... Hapu		49	Hapu
64	... utab	99	... ka Xenu		50	Shemsu
65	Raherab	100	... ka Heburn		51	Menu
66	Ranebsen	101	Lost		52	Ur

67	Lost	102	Ra ...		129	... bebra
68	Ra	103	Raha		130	Lost
69	Rasheperen	104	Raha		131	Lost
70	Radadkheru	105	Rases		132	Lost
71	Rasankh	106	Ranebatiau			
72	Ranefertum ...	107	Rapebatinu			
73	Rasekhem ...	108	Rasmen			
74	Rakaab?	109	Rasenser		116	Lost
75	Raneferab	110	Rahashed			Summation

111	Raha		
112	Lost		73 kings in all

Of the remaining kings in Petrie's list, 117-120 probably belong to Dynasty xv
133-142 to Dynasty xvii, and possibly 121-124 to Dynasty xvi.

(To face page 13)

DYNASTY XIV. (XOITE), 76 KINGS; 184 YEARS (AFR.),
484 (EUS.)

(See Table facing this page.)

These kings, with their average reigns of $2\frac{1}{2}$ years each, come, no doubt, immediately before xv. : this brings them exactly parallel with xii. if with Manetho we reckon Usertesen i. as the first king. I cannot hesitate in assigning their position as viceroys or vassals of Dyn. xii. By its kings they were established, with them they disappear; bequeathing to us one scarab, that of Raneferab, and a very doubtful cartouche of the same king. That 184 years should have elapsed thus silently is not even credible to modern end-to-end chronologers; who begin invariably (and this is the only thing they do agree in) by indorsing Mariette's statement that "monumental proofs are superabundant and have been collected in great numbers by Egyptologers, which demonstrate that all the royal races enumerated by Manetho occupied the throne one after another"; but with hardly an exception make the dynasties from xiv. to xvii. more or less contemporary. I need hardly say that the so-called proofs of their hypothesis by De Rougé and others were valid against the making overlaps of i.–iii. and iv.–vi. as Wilkinson and the earlier school of English chronologers did; but are utterly valueless in such instances as viii., xiv. and xvi., where no monumental datum has been discovered, and for the others, ix.–xi., xiii.–xvii., this arbitrary dictum has been disregarded in practice

[To face pag. 13]

Of the remaining kings in Petrie's list, 117–120 probably belong to Dynasty xv.; 133–142 to Dynasty xvii., and possibly 121–124 to Dynasty xvi.

DYNASTY XIV. (XOITE), 76 KINGS; 184 YEARS (AFR.), 484 (EUS.)

(See Table facing this page.)

These kings, with their average reigns of $2\frac{1}{2}$ years each, come, no doubt, immediately before xv. : this brings them exactly parallel with xii. if with Manetho we reckon Usertesen i. as the first king. I cannot hesitate in assigning their position as viceroys or vassals of Dyn. xii. By its kings they were established, with them ·they disappear; bequeathing to us one scarab, that of Raneferab, and a very doubtful cartouche of the same king. That 184 years should have elapsed thus silently is not even credible to modern end-to-end chronologers; who begin invariably (and this is the only thing they do agree in) by indorsing Mariette's statement that "monumental proofs are superabundant and have been collected in great numbers by Egyptologers, which demonstrate that all the royal races enumerated by Manetho occupied the throne one after another"; but with hardly an exception make the dynasties from xiv. to xvii. more or less contemporary. I need hardly say that the so-called proofs of their hypothesis by De Rougé and others were valid against the making overlaps of i.–iii. and iv.–vi. as Wilkinson and the earlier school of English chronologers did; but are utterly valueless in such instances as viii., xiv. and xvi., where no monumental datum has been discovered, and for the others, ix.–xi., xiii.–xvii., this arbitrary dictum has been disregarded in practice by every eminent Egyptologer, however strongly he may maintain it in theory.

DYN. XV.—(*See Table facing this page.*)

In the Turin list, after a summation, which must be that of xiv., as no other can be made to fit, we find 117 Ra·user..., 118 Ra·user... for the first two kings of xv. The earlier of these was doubtless Ra·s·user·en Khyan the heq Setu who conquered the Delta, ejected the native kings (xiii.) from Memphis, and set up his statue in the temple at Bubastis. He is clearly the same personage as Saites (or Khaites, compare Khufu = Soufis) the heq Shasa, who lived at Memphis, rendered the upper and lower regions of Egypt tributary, and occupied the Bubastite channel. The occurrence of two such exactly similar conquests by Eastern chiefs could never have passed unnoticed. The second was probably Rauserkha, who, as well as Khyan, has by some been placed in Dyn. ix., where there is certainly no place for either of these Orientals among the native Herakleopolites. Appa·aa·qnen may easily have been transliterated into Apakhnan, and I know no other name that could be; but in this instance the order in Josephus is certainly wrong, Aausera was the earlier of the two.

St·aa·n is, I think, a transliteration of Set·aa·nub (in full Set·aa·pehti Nubti·set : but shorter forms Set·pehti, Set·nub also occur) from whose epoch the 400 years was reckoned by Ramessu ii. of which more hereafter ; and Aaseh is a very likely origin for Assis. How the names Salatis and Benon were obtained I cannot at present conjecture : Janias may

DYNASTY XV. SHEPHERDS (HYKSOS).

B.C.	ADOPTED	YEARS	JOSEPHUS	YEARS	AFR.	YEARS	REN. XVII.
1840	1. Rasuseren Khyan	19	1. Salatis	19, 0	1. Saites	19	19
1821	2. Rauser [Kha]	44	2. Beon	44, 0	2. Bnon	44	40
1777	3. Apepa Aauserra	61	4. Apofis	61, 0	3. Pakhnan	61	
1716	4. Apepa Aaqnenra	37	3. Apakhnas	36, 7	4. Staan	50	
1679	5. Setaanub	50	5. Junias	50, 1	5. Arkhles	49	30
1629	6. Aasehra	49	6. Assis	49, 2	6. Apofis	61	14
1580	Sum	260		259, 10		284	103

A variant is given by Synkellos :

	JOS.	MAN.
5. Sethos	50	50
6. Kertos	29	44
7. Asoth	20	24

but his quotations are not confirmed by our extant texts of Josephus or Manetho.

[To face page 44.

be Aanub: and Arkhles looks like a variant of Herakles (Har·ka·ra). So much for the names.

As for the history: there is no trace of any possession of Southern Egypt by Salatis as Josephus says there is; and no monument of the two first kings: the possession of Thebes and the South was probably not obtained till 1731 when xvii. was set up as tributary to the Hyksos in the reign of Apepa i., whom we meet with as a builder as far south as Gebelen. There is a mathematical papyrus of his 33rd year, 1744 B.C. In the 17th year according to the tradition preserved by Synkellos, Joseph was made Shalit of all Egypt. This would make Jacob's descent from Palestine fall in the 26th year, 1772–1 B.C., and from this time to the Exodus of the lepers (identified with the Hebrews by Manetho) is exactly 430 years as stated in Exodus xii. 40.

Under Apepa ii. the Theban viceroys began to be restive, but this may be more fitly treated later on. In the time of Aseth (but rather of Assis = Aaseh) according to Synkellos the 5 Epacts were added to the year. This is far too late; they were in use from the beginning of Dyn. xii.: what this epoch really means I will try to show when I treat of the Sed festivals.

The erroneous statements of the years in the Manethonic lists require some explanation. The "4 Kings and 103 years" of Eusebius are certainly taken from the Chronicler's Dyn. vi., which he mistook for xvii. as already explained; for the same reason he shifts the place of the dynasty, this being the only one he could make of sufficiently low amount to get in the Chronicler's successive numbers 190, 103, 348, which he assigns to xvi., xvii., xviii. His violent alterations to this end are too palpable to require further notice here; and I shall have to recur to them when I treat of his scheme in its entirety. The numbers in Africanus must be considered in connexion with those in xii., where there is a deficiency of 24 years, exactly counterbalancing the excess of 24 here. I have no hesitation in attributing the alteration to Africanus himself. He placed his date for the Exodus in the first year of Khebros, near the beginning of xviii. instead of the end, and he wanted the tradition that Joseph was made Shalit in the 17th of Apofis to agree with his reckoning of 215 years from the descent of Jacob (26 Apofis) to the Exodus. He apparently reckoned thus:

26 Apofis to end	. .	35 years
Dynasty xvii.	. .	151 „
Amosis	. . . .	25 „
Sum	.	211 „

This is 4 years in error; and this error is duly chronicled by Synkellos. Note, however, that Africanus makes no account of xvi., nor does any chronologer till quite recent times. Having got Apofis into position, whether accidentally or designedly, he crosses out the wrong years for that king's true place, leaving Pakhnan 61 instead of 37; thus introducing an error of 24 years counterbalanced by the 8 instead of 32 in xii. Manetho had doubtless 184 years for xii., and *teste Josepho* 260 for xv.

DYNASTY XVI. (HYKSOS). 32 HELLENIC SHEPHERDS,
518 YEARS (AFR.); 5 THEBANS, 190 YEARS (EUS.).

Here, again, Eusebius' statement of 190 years is taken from the Chronicler and has no historical authority whatever. It has, however, afforded so convenient a loophole for modern chronologers to escape from another gap of 518 years of absolute vacuum, during which the monuments are completely silent, that the majority of them have adopted it, and, ignoring Africanus' statement that this dynasty was composed of shepherds, have, contrary to their end-to-end principles, made it a long-reign Theban dynasty contemporary with xv. It is really a slight variant of Josephus' statement (quoted from Manetho) that the 6 kings of xv. "and their successors" occupied Egypt 511 years: by which he means not that they had supreme rule for that time, but that these years elapsed before their final expulsion. The 518 years are made up thus:

Dynasty xv.	. . . .	260 years
Dynasty xvi. contemporary with xviii. 1–14	.	245 „
Osarsif, during the flight of Amenofath	. .	13 „

Africanus calls xv. Phœnicians and xvi. Hellenes: but Josephus has "some say they were Arabians," and every indication of race and language points to their having been really so—Arabian Semites from the Syrian desert.

Is it then merely accidental coincidence that an Arabian dynasty of exactly 245 years occurs in Berosus just at this date for whom no place can be found in the canon of Kings of Babylon? I think hardly so; the coincidences of time and name are too exact, and therefore, rash as the conjecture may seem, I venture to give as the list of Dyn. xvi.:

1–6	As in Dynasty xv.	1840 B.C.	260 years
7	Mardokentes	1580 ,,	45 ,,
8	Wanting	1535 ,,	[20] ,,
9	Sisimardakos	1515 ,,	28 ,,
10	Nabius	1487 ,,	37 ,,
11	Parannus	1450 ,,	40 ,.
12	Nabonnabus	1410 ,,	25 ,,
13–15	Wanting	1385 ,,	[50] ,,
16	Osarsif	1335 ,,	13 ,,
	Exodus of lepers	1332 ,,	518 years

The conjectural [20] is filled in so as to make 3 pairs of reigns, $45 + 20 = 28 + 37 = 40 + 25 = 65$. The numbers are clearly artificial.

The kings	91	lost		121	A .. f
	92	lost		122	Set ...
	93	?		123	Sunn ...
	94	A ...		124	Hor ...
	95	A ...			(Petrie's numeration)

usually placed in Dyn. xiv. may belong to xvi.; but this is very doubtful. The strongest argument in its favour is that the names begin with A and Set.

DYN. XVII.—*(See Table facing this page.)*

The names under Monuments (except ...zefa) are from the tombs at Thebes; "...zefa" and Turin years from a fragment of the papyrus, which fits well in here, but is generally placed with Dyn. iv., where it does not fit at all. Petrie has ably refuted this unfortunate hypothesis, but others still put it

DYNASTY XVII. 43 DIOSPOLITES AND 43 SHEPHERDS, 151 YEARS (AFR.).

THIS IS EUSEBIUS' XVIII. DYNASTY OF DIOSPOLITES, 250 YEARS.

MONUMENTS.	ADOPTED.	TURIN.	SOTHIS.	YEARS.	B.C.
1.	[10]				
2. ... zefa	6	6	Khamois	12	1731
3.	6	6			1721
4.	24	24	Miamous	14	1715
5. Squenra Taaa i.	24	24	Amesesis	65	1709
6.	23	23	(ancestors of Aahmes)		1685
7.	8	8			1661
8. Squenra Taaa ii. Aa	27		Onses (Aasu)	50	1638
9. Squenra Taaa iii. Ken	15				1630
10. Kames	8				1603
11. Skhentnebra					1588
Sum	151			141	
Sum of 2–7	91	91		91	1580

[To face page 48.]

forward as unquestionable. He, however, assigns the
fragment to Dyn. xvi. The other year-column and
names are from the book of the Sothis. The sums
of these two reckonings exactly coincide. Tiaa i.
was cotemporary with Apepa Aaqenenra according
to the tale of Apepa and Seqenenra (Sall. Pap. i.).
There is no evidence that the three Tiaas were
successive; or that the intervening kings, if any,
were of the same family as they. They certainly
had not the same burying place. Petrie (ii. p. 3)
has given an elaborate chronological table of the last
century of this dynasty. I therefore insert one here
for comparison.

B.C.	
1685 (?)	Tiaa i. reigns.
1630 (?)	Tiaa Aa ii. reigns.
1626	Tiaaken iii. born.
1626	Aahhotep born.
1611	Aahhotep marries (ætat. 15).
1610	Kames (her son) born.
1609	Skhentneb (her son) born.
	Then 2 more children.
1606	Aahmes born.
1605	Tiaaken (ætat. 23) marries Aahhotep (ætat. 21).
1604	Nefertari born.
	Then 8 other children.
1588	Tiaaken dies (ætat. 40). Kames succeeds (ætat. 22). Aahmes (ætat. 18) marries Nefertari (ætat. 16).
1580	Kames dies (ætat. 30), Aahmes succeeds (ætat. 26).
1555	Aahmes dies (ætat. 51), Amenhotep succeeds (ætat. 25).
1523	Amenhotep dies. ? Aahhotep alive (ætat. 98).

The chief differences from Petrie's table are, first,
I take Aahmes's age at death to be 51; Petrie
(ii. p. 2) says that "about 55" is one of his "fixed
points." Compare p. 335, where he admits that he

D

may have been only just over 50. Secondly, while admitting that Aahhotep was alive in the 10th year of Amenhotep i., *i.e.*, in 1545, when she was 81 years old, I think (but with submission to more skilled authority) that the evidence of the Iufi stele as to her living to 100 is very dubious.

I regard the "43 Shepherd Kings" in Africanus as an interpolation. Manetho may have had a statement that this dynasty was cotemporary with the Shepherds; but both the 43's are discordant with the historical facts. I shall treat of these numbers further on.

The Turin number for the sixth king has also been read 21 and 33; as either of these numbers would, if adopted, only require a readjustment of the previous reigns of which there are no historical facts known, the doubt as to the reading is of no import at present.

ON THE HYKSOS, B.C. 1840-1580.

We are now prepared to consider the narrative of the Hyksos invasion as extracted by Josephus from Manetho. In the time of Timaios (Tmaa, Amenemhat iii.) ignoble men came up from the East, invaded the country, and subdued it without a battle B.C. *c.* 1856. After some sixteen years of insidious concentration of their power during the time of Amenemhat iv. and Queen Sebekneferu, in 1840 they made one of themselves king — viz., Salatis (Saites, Khyan, Rasuseren). He seized Bubastis, Tanis, and all the eastern part of the Delta, expelling therefrom Dyn. xiii., who under the

earlier Sebekhoteps, &c., had occupied those towns.
They fell back on Thebes, put an end to the enfeebled
twelfth dynasty, and fixed their residence sometimes
in Thebes, sometimes in the Fayum. The royal
abode of Salatis was at Memphis, but at Avaris on
the east of the Bubastite channel in the Saite nome,
which he rebuilt and fortified, he during the summer
collected his tribute, paid his troops, and exercised
the garrison. For Saite perhaps we should read the
nome of Supti. The usual emendation of Sethroite
and the identification of Avaris with Tanis are
very doubtful. Josephus says he rendered both the
upper and lower regions of Egypt tributary, but
neither his reign nor that of his successor has left
any trace on the Theban monuments, not even an
inscription of a Hyksos name or a usurpation of a
Theban cartouche. It is at Bubastis, Tanis, and
Memphis in the North, at Gebelen in the South,
that we find monumental evidence of Hyksos kings.
Thebes they have not yet; the Fayum, as far as I
can make out, they never occupied at all. Having
got the Delta, their next attack was on Herakleopolis.
I conjecture that they conquered Dyn. ix. somewhere
about 1765–60, and established a new dynasty (x.)
of vassals. The exceptionally long reigns of these
kings point to a quiet indolence on their part; they
could not have shared in the war which the Hyksos
waged upon the Egyptians "during the whole period
of their (fifteenth) dynasty" in hope of exterminating
them.

If the tradition that Joseph "stood before
Pharaoh" in the 17th year of Apofis, 1761 B.C.,

be correct, and there is not a shadow of evidence
against it, and the numbers are greatly in its favour,
this would come just about his time.

Following up the same policy against Thebes as
against Herakleopolis, I suppose that Apepa dislodged
Dyn. xiii. from that province, and set up Dyn. xvii.
as vassals. In this instance we know what the
actual condition of the Government was from the
tale of Apepa and Seqenenra. " There was no lord
and king . . . Seqenenra was ur or heq (vassal) in
the South . . . Apepi was sar (suzerain) in Havar."
I suppose that the status was similar under Dyn. x.
in Herakleopolis, but not under xiii. in the Fayum, as
there is no indication of any break in this dynasty,
at which we can suppose it to have come under the
domination of the Hyksos, who would certainly have
set up a new line of vassal princes. The time during
which Apepa ii. and Seqenenra were contemporary
was 1685-79; this fixes the date of the incidents of
the tale. " When they " (the Hyksos), says Josephus,
" had our rulers in their hands, they burnt our cities,
demolished the temples of the gods, and inflicted
every kind of barbarity on the inhabitants, slaying
some, and reducing the wives and children of others
to a state of slavery." Moreover, King Apepa made
Sutekh lord instead of Ra, and " the foreign hordes
of the Amu destroyed the ancient works, being
ignorant of the god Ra," says Queen Hatshepsut in
her inscription at Beni Hassan. She says no word
of any mischief in Thebes, but only states " there
had been Amu in the midst of the Delta and in
Havar." This is just what one would expect if my

view of this usurpation be right, but far from it if
Salatis took the whole country at once as commonly
supposed. This oppression at last became unendur-
able, and under Seqenenra Tiaaken a rebellion took
place, followed by "a long and mighty war." This
king was slain in battle 1588, but his successor Al·is·-
fr·ag·mu·thosis (Ra·uaz·khpr·ka·mes) shut them up
in Havar 1587. Then there was a junction between
xvii. and xiii. ("the kings of the Thebans and the
rest of Egypt") under Aahmes, son of Kames, who
laid siege to Havar (Hatuar, in the tomb inscription
of Admiral Aahmes at Elkab), and accepted its unexpected capitulation in 1580, the year of his
father's death, his own accession, and the epoch of
the eighteenth Dyn., of which he was the first king.
Much confusion is introduced into this account by
some modern writers by identifying the Thummosis
of Josephus with Tahutmes i. ; but this Thummosis
or Tethmosis is certainly the Amoses of Eusebius,
and therefore the Amos of Africanus. The length of
his reign, 25 years, 4 months, is sufficient to prove
this, to say nothing of the inextricable muddle in
which we become involved on any other hypothesis.

Dyn. x. does not appear to have submitted to
xviii. till 1580; the Herakleopolites seem not to
have taken any part in this war. I append a tabular
compilation of the events of this time.

	XV.	IX.-X.	XII.	XIII.
1853	Hyk. in Egypt		7. Amenemhat iv.	in Delta
1840	1. Khyan		8. Queen S. dies	at Thebes
1821	2. Benon			
1777	3. Apepa i.			
1765-60		x. established		
1761	Joseph Shalit			
1752	Jacob Eisode			
1731			xvii. established	in Fayum
1716	4. Apepa ii.			
1685-79	Apepa and		5. Seqenenra	
1679	5. Setaanub			
1629	6. Aaseh			
1587	{ Shut up in Havar }		xvii. revolts	{ joins with xvii.
1580	xv. expelled	x. joins xviii.	xviii. 1. Aahmes	
1555			2. Amenhotep i.	

DYN. XVIII.—(*See Table facing this page.*)

Before giving the years for these kings, it is necessary to determine their identity, as the Manethonic lists are evidently disarranged. All three of them, however, agree in their order, and must have come from a common source. I will take them in this order : 1. Tethmosis certainly = Amos(es) = Aahmes, and cannot be Tahutmes i. ; Josephus has mistaken the name. 2. Khebron must be Kheperen—*i.e.*, Tahutmes ii. 3. Amenofis is of course Amenhotep i. 4. Queen Amersis (Maara), "his sister" (Josephus), can only be Hatshepsut, sister of Tahutmes ii., not of Amenofis. This proves that the Manethonic order is wrong. 5. Misfragmuthosis must be Menkheper-kara Tahutmes iii., the "g" therein representing "ka"; he cannot be an Amenhotep. 6. Mefres or Misfris ought therefore to be Menkheprura Tahutmes iv. ;

DYNASTY XVIII. (DIOSPOLITE.)

ABYDOS AND MONUMENTS.		JOSEPHUS.	AFRICANUS.	EUSEBIUS.
1. Nebpehtira	Aahmes	1. Tethmosis	Amos	Amoses
2. Zeserkara	Amenhotep i.	2. Khebron	Khebros	Khebron
3. Aakheperkara	Tahutmes i.	3. Amenofis	Amenofthis	Am[en]ofis
4. Aakheperenra	Tahutmes ii.	4. Amesses	Amersis	[Amesses]
Maakara	Hatshepsut	5. Mefres	Misafris	Memfres
5. Menkheperkara	Tahutmes iii.	6. Meframuthosis	Misfragmuthosis	Mysfarmuthosis
6. Aakheprura	Amenhotep ii.	7. Thmosis	Tuthmosis	Tuthmosis
7. Menkheprura	Tahutmes iv.	8. Amenofis	Amenofis	Amenofis
8. Nebmaara	Amenhotep iii.	9. Oros	Oros	Oros
Neferkheprura	Amenhotep iv.	10. Akenkhres	Akherres	Akhenkheres
Neterhekuast	Akhenaten			
Ankhkheprura	Rasmenkhka	11. Rathotis	Rathos	[Rathotis]
Rakhepruneb	Amentutankh	12. Akenkheres i.	Khebres	Kherres
Rakheperkhepru	Armaat Ay	13. Akenkheres ii.	Akherres	Akherres
9. Kaserkhepru	Horemheb	14. Armais	Armeses	Armais
		15. Ramesses	Ramesses	Ramesses
10. Menpehtira	Ramessu i.	Armesses	Amenofath	Amenofis
		16. Amenofis		

[To face page 51.

he seems, however, from the years assigned him to have been interchanged (for name only, not years) with Tuthmosis or Tahutmes i. by a further corruption. 8. Amenofis must be Amenhotep ii. 9. Oros is fixed by his regnal years as Amenhotep iii. 11. Rathotis is of necessity Ra...tut (ankhamen). 10, 12, 13. Akhenres Khebres Kherres (levelled down to Akenkheres by Josephus) will be Akhenkheprura Ankhkheprura and Aykheperkhepru. 14. Armais is admitted to be Horemheb. 15. Ramesses is Ramessu i. ; and 16, Amenofath is for the present doubtful.

Petrie says the name Mefres is "fixed" to Thotmes iii. by Pliny. Pliny is not so accurate as to be incapable of mistaking Mefres for Meframuthosis (Mefres Touthmosis).

Eusebius places Akherres before Kherres; but Africanus and Josephus are clearly right in their order.

Having thus got a probably true order for Manetho's list, the next step is to test it by the regnal years; but I will just premise a word as to how this dislocated order arose.

I believe that the original arrangement was as follows; the numbers indicate the kings in the order in which they have reached us.

1, 3, 5	12, 11
2, 4, 6	13, 14
8, 7	16, 15
9, 10	

If these be taken line after line, the kings will succeed in the order in which I have placed them, viz., that of the monuments, but Manetho's copyists have taken the first two lines as three columns, and read the other five *boustrophedon* from right to left and left to right alternately as the consecution of the numbers sufficiently indicates. This fundamental error must have arisen in a Greek, not an Egyptian list.

DYNS. XVIII. AND XIX.—(*See Table facing this page.*)

The monumental years given are minima ; some months (from 1 to 11) in defect. Mahler's calculation from New Moons, &c., of the epoch of Tahutmes iii. is the foundation stone of Egyptian chronology : it supplies a fixed era from which to calculate in either direction, and is the only one we have at present. He has, however, made a slip by interpreting his results in Julian years ; they should be in vague years. Eisenlohr has corrected this (Biblical Archæological Society, 1895) ; I append his corrections.

EVENT.	DATE.	MAHLER.	EISENLOHR.
Coronation of Thotmes iii.	4 Pakhons, 1 T. iii.	1503 Mar. 20	1504 May 4
New Moon	21 Pakhons, 23 T. iii.	1481 April 5	1482 May 16
New Moon	30 Mekhir 24 T. iii.	1479 Jan. 15	1480 Feb. 24
Death of Thotmes iii.	30 Famenoth, 54 T. iii.	1449 Feb. 14	1450 [Mar.] 18

Another epoch of which there can be scarcely any doubt (I am obliged here to anticipate my discussion on Seds and Sothics, to which please to refer) is that of Menofres (Menpehra Ramessu i.), the beginning of

DYNASTIES XVIII., XIX. (DIOSPOLITE.)

DYNASTIES XVIII. XIX. (DIOSPOLITE.)

Monuments	Years	Manetho	Arm.	Eus.	Jos.	Cast.	B.C.
XVIII.							
1. Aahmes	21+	Amos	21	25	25, 4	25, 4	1580
2. Amenhotep i.	x	Amenofthis	12	21	20, 7	20, 7	1562
3. Aakheper T. i.	x	Mefres	12	12	13, 9	13, 9	1534
4. Khepera T. ii.	21	Khebron	13	[13]	13, 0	13, 0	1515
5. Maakra II.	21	Amesses	[21]	[21]	21, 9	21, 9	1562
6. Menkheperka T. iii	54	Meframuthosis	26	26	26, 10	26, 10	1481
7. Amenhotep ii.	25	Amenofis	9	31	30, 10	30, 10	1450
8. Tahutmes iv.	7	Thmosis	9	9	9, 8	9, 8	1450
9. Oros	7	Oros	28	38	36, 5	36, 5	1414
10. Amenhotep iii.	36	Akherres	32	12	12, 1	12, 1	1421
11. Khepura A. iv.	16	Khebres	6	[9]	12, 0	12, 0	1374
12. Ankhkhepura		Rathotis	9	9			1362
13. Ratnt		Akherres	12	8	12, 3	12, 3	1359
14. Khepru Ay		Armis	5	5	4, 1	4, 1	1350
15. Horemheb	28	Amenofath	19	40	19, 6	19, 6	1343
(Merephra	29						1328
(Ramesu i.	1	Ramesses	1	68	1, 4	1, 4	1318
		Sum (stated 263)	262	348	266, 10	262, 10	
		(Omitted Armosses Miamun			66, 0	66, 0	
		Sum stated			263, 0		
XIX.							
1. Seti i.		Sethos	51	55	59	51	1327
2. Rameses ii.	66	Rhapsaces	61	66	66	66	1274
		Sum to here	474	469	518	473	
3. Seti Merenptah	22	Amenoefthes	20	8	Sixt.	21	1207
4. Amenmeses		Ammenemes	5	26	26	5	1187
5. Siptah		Thuoris	7	7	7	7	1174
6. Seti ii.		(Okhyras Nekhepsos)	14	14	14	14	1167
7. Nekhtsit			19		19	19	1163
8. Rameses iii		Rhamses	1			22	1144
		Sum of xix.	594	102			
		Stated	209	194		209	1198

[To face page 56.]

the Sothic cycle in 1318. Moreover, the agreement between the Chronicler and Manetho in a total of 472 years for xviii. and xix. (244+228, and 263+ 209), although they divided these dynasties at a different epoch, shows that the sum stated in Africanus for xviii. (263 years) is the right one. The dynasty began therefore in 1580. There are then 6 years omitted in Josephus and Eusebius somewhere in the first 4 reigns. I have added them to Tahutmes i., the copy of whose reign seems to have been confused with that of his successor. Again, the reign of Amenhotep must certainly be increased by 4 years at least, as his seventeenth year is mentioned in the monuments. This gives an excess of 10 years for the first 10 kings in Josephus, which I correct (following Maspero)* by cancelling 10 years in Smenkhka. Josephus has still left an excess of 4 years in his sum, but Eusebius has 8 years for Ay against his 12. Adopting this, our corrected column comes out exactly right by emending 4 reigns in the years (the months I have kept most scrupulously), of which alterations two are necessitated by facts, one has good ancient authority, and one still better though modern.

* The Chronicler, however, whose text probably ran thus:
[9] Diospolites, 194 years
5 [Diospolites, 50 years],
seems to have reckoned 12 y. 5 m. for Ankhkhepru, and there are indications of co-regencies between Thotmes iv. and Amenhotep iii.; Am. iii. and Am. iv. The 12 y. 5 m. may therefore be correct, and the 10 years excess have to be compensated by the co-regencies. If so, the epochs of Am. iii., iv. will have to be thrown back a few years but no argument in the text will in any way be affected. The Seds all come right in either case.

the Sothic cycle in 1318. Moreover, the agreement between the Chronicler and Manetho in a total of 472 years for xviii. and xix. (244+228, and 263+ 209), although they divided these dynasties at a different epoch, shows that the sum stated in Africanus for xviii. (263 years) is the right one. The dynasty began therefore in 1580. There are then 6 years omitted in Josephus and Eusebius somewhere in the first 4 reigns. I have added them to Tahutmes i., the copy of whose reign seems to have been confused with that of his successor. Again, the reign of Amenhotep must certainly be increased by 4 years at least, as his seventeenth year is mentioned in the monuments. This gives an excess of 10 years for the first 10 kings in Josephus, which I correct (following Maspero)* by cancelling 10 years in Smenkhka. Josephus has still left an excess of 4 years' in his sum, but Eusebius has 8 years for Ay against his 12. Adopting this, our corrected column comes out exactly right by emending 4 reigns in the years (the months I have kept most scrupulously), of which alterations two are necessitated by facts, one has good ancient authority, and one still better though modern.

* The Chronicler, however, whose text probably ran thus:

[9] Diospolites, 194 years

5 [Diospolites, 50 years],

seems to have reckoned 12 y. 5 m. for Ankhkhepru, and there are indications of co-regencies between Thotmes iv. and Amenhotep iii.; Am. iii. and Am. iv. The 12 y. 5 m. may therefore be correct, and the 10 years excess have to be compensated by the co-regencies. If so, the epochs of Am. iii., iv. will have to be thrown back a few years but no argument in the text will in any way be affected. The Seds all come right in either case.

Turning to Eusebius, his exaggerated sum (taken from Chronicle vii.–x.) and his reason for falsifying this and other dynasties will be more conveniently treated of as a whole under the head of Schemes. He follows Josephus for Thotmes i., but his 28 years for Oros are difficult to understand. It would be easy to explain 4 years of the deficit by supposing a co-regnancy between him and his successor, but not 8 or 9, and there is no likelihood of a co-regnancy with his predecessor. Possibly we should read 38 here and 5 for Khebres. Anyhow, the sum must be kept as 348 ; and as the insertion of the two missing reigns exactly makes this up, there can be no question that they should be inserted as I have placed them in brackets.

Africanus' is in this instance the most corrupt of all the lists ; the motive is explained under the head of Schemes. He has cancelled the years of Amos, but left the telltale name showing that they were given in his author : he follows Josephus as to Tahutmes i., and understates Rathotis, thus creating a deficit of $25 + 6 + 3 = 34$. On the other side he over-estimates Amenhotep i., iv., Smenkh, and Ay by $3 + 16 + 10 + 4 = 33$. These are clearly artificial alterations needing no further notice as yet.

All the lists concur in abbreviating Tahutmes i., lengthening Smenkh, and transposing Th. iii. with Am. ii. The original muddling of this dynasty was evidently due to Josephus. Subsequent Christian chronologers edited and " improved " his version.

MONTH-DATES.—(*See Table facing this page.*)

MONTH-DATES.

B.C.	KINGS.	YEARS.	MONTH-DATES.	MONTH.	EVENT.
1580	Aahmes	25, 4	c. 1 Tybi	v.	Accession
1555	Am. i.	20, 7	c. 1 Pakhons	ix.	Accession
1547			9 Epifi	xi.	Sed festival in 9th year
1535	Th. i.	18, 9	21 Famenoth	vii.	Coronation before death of Am. i.
1534		13, 0	c. 1 Khoiak	iv.	Accession: Sed [16 Epifi 1519]
1515	Th. ii. and Hat.		c. 1 Thoth	i.	Accession: epoch of Hat.
1504		21, 9	4 Pakhons	ix.	Coronation and epoch of Th. iii.
1502	Hat. and Th. iii.		1 Thoth	i.	Accession
1499		30, 10	[21 Epifi]	xi.	Sed in 16th of Hat.
1481	Tb. iii.		c. 30 Pakhons	ix.	Accession
1471		25, 10	28 Epifi	xi.	Sed in 3rd. of Th. iii.
1450	Am. ii.	9, 8	30 Famenoth	vii.	Accession: Sed [7 Mesore 1435]
1424	Th. iv.		c. 30 Tybi	v.	Accession
1414	Am. iii.	36, 5	13 Epifi	xi.	Coronation
1378		16, 1	c. 30 Thoth	i.	Accession: Sed [14 Mesore 1407]
1362	Am. iv.	2, 5	c. 30 Mekhir	vi.	
1359	Smenkh	9, 0	c. 30 Famenoth	vii.	
1350	Ratnt	8, 3	c. 30 Mesore	xii.	Sed [28 Mesore 1351]
1343	Ay	23, 7	c. 30 Mesore	xii.	
1318	Hor	1, 4	c. 30 Athyr	iii.	
1317	R. i.		c. 30 Payni	x.	
			c. 30 Paofi	ii.	17 Sep. Julian

[To face page 58.

For this dynasty, and for no other, we have (thanks to Josephus) the month-dates of accession, which must have been given for all the dynasties in Manetho's original list, just as they were in the Turin papyrus. We have also monumental inscriptions of Seds and coronation days. I have gathered all these into one table. The monumental dates are given in the column of "month-dates" literally copied: the accession dates calculated from Josephus have c. (circa) prefixed, because the days not being given there may be an error of one or two at most in the number of months reckoned in particular instances. For instance, 1450 B.C. Famenoth 30 is a certain date: calculating back to 1582 by Josephus' numbers would, if the months were exact, lead to 30 Mesore. But the monuments give 1 Thoth, six days difference, the 5 Epacts intervening, which enables me to correct the error arising from the omission of the days. In other instances there is no such check available.

One important result from this table is that wherever a monumental record of a coronation has been found the coronation date precedes that of accession. This had been recognised in the case of Thotmes iii., where Petrie, for instance, admits that his coronation preceded the death of Thotmes ii. by 3 months. The true interval as shown by Josephus' numbers was 15 months. But in the case of Thotmes i., crowned seven months before the death of Amenhotep i., and in that of Amenhotep iii., crowned 2 (?) months before the death of Thotmes iv., it has been generally assumed that the coronation was after the accession. It is not possible to make the two sets of numbers consistent on this hypothesis.

Another result is that the Sed dates are shown to be in agreement with other known dates. Thus, in the case of Amenhotep i., 8y. 2m. elapsed between his accession and the Sed. Only 8 years can therefore be allowed in a reckoning where the months are not given, and this brings the Sed year to 1547, not 1546, as usually reckoned. This is as it should be.

Again, in the case of Ratut the Sed falls on 28 Mesore, 1351, a year anterior to the accession of Ay : this also comes right. I do not know of any other system in which the Sed dates all fall in their proper reigns.

If the reader be unfamiliar with calculations of this kind, I must ask him to refer to the subsequent section of "Sothics and Seds." These could not be treated of till the dynasties had all been examined, and it would be superfluous to give explanations twice over. It is awkward to have to arrange one's matter in this way, but it is inevitable here without falling into greater difficulties.

For Dyn. xix. the Sed date in the second year of Merenptah fixes his accession to 1207–8 ; the length of the reign of Ramessu ii. is known to be 66–7 years. Seti i. must therefore have reigned 43–4 years. Merenptah was co-regnant with Ramessu ii. for 12 years, and if we give him 22 years alone the sum of the three reigns is 132, agreeing with Africanus: there is no objection known to 5 and

7 years for the next kings; and 65 for Rhamses, which must have been the number altered by 5 years by Africanus to 60, as shown by the discrepancy between the actual and stated sums, is made up of $14+19+32=65$. The 14 and 19 are taken from the Mestræan list in Synkellos, our only authority for these kings' reigns. I can see no objection to them. Many good authorities, however, who admit gaps in the monumental records elsewhere of centuries, are scandalised at the idea of a few units being in this instance passed over by them in silence.

Rhamses must be out of place in Africanus, and I follow E. de Rougé for the order of the last 3 kings: if the order of Chabas with Seti ii. immediately after Merenptah be preferred it will in no way interfere with my argument.

The 26 years in Eusebius and Synkellos is probably derived from the addition of $5 + 7 + 14 = 26$. We have met with similar sophistications in earlier dynasties: but the sum 194 in Eusebius is taken direct from the corrupted Chronicle list, as his sums have been for the three dynasties preceding. He has altered the numbers for Seti and Merenptah to suit this sum of 194, and has then transferred Ramessu iii. to Dyn. xx., as many modern authorities do. He has, however, in his usual careless way subtracted 32 years, the time of the sole reign of Ramessu iii., and added to Dyn. xx. 37 years, including his co-regnancy with Ramessu iv., thus getting $135+37=172$. It seems at first sight strange to end a dynasty in the middle of a reign, but on the hypothesis of contemporary dynasties there is no difficulty. The beginning of Dyn. xxi., and not that of Dyn. xx., fixes the date of the loss of supremacy of Dyn. xix. On the end to end hypothesis the numbers in Africanus cannot be explained ; nor do I know that any attempt at explanation has been made. It is so much easier to assume that all refractory numbers are Christian forgeries.

I must add a word on the singular dislocation in the Mestræan list.

That Amenses, who is expressly identified by Synkellos with Amenemes, is out of place is certain : and that Okhyras (Userra or Userkheperra) is identical with Seti ii. is most probable : the identity of name ; the number of years, 14, which with 32 for Ramessu iii. and 19 for Nekhepsos, makes up the 65 required for the Rhamses of Africanus ; and the fact that if Okhyras be not Seti ii., then Seti ii. is omitted altogether, leave little room for doubt. The original arrangement was probably in columns :

| (1) 55. Amenses | (2) 49. Thouosis |
| (3) 56. Okhyras | (4) 50. Nekhepsos |

But when the final linear arrangement was adopted Amenses and Okhyras in the first column were at first omitted, and then, the chronological arrangement being quite misunderstood, they were thrown in at the end of Dyn. xx.

ON THE DATE OF THE EXODUS.

Eusebius places the Exodus in 1511, the first year of Akherres (Khebres, Afr.) and last of Rhathos ; he reckons 215 years from Abraham's call to the Eisode of Jacob in the eleventh year of Apofis and 215 for the sojourn in Egypt. As all his numbers for Dyn. xvi.–xix. are taken from dynasties of the Chronicler misplaced, we need trouble no further about his absurd hypothesis, which has no foundation beyond the similarity of the transliterations, Khebres xviii. 12 and Khebros xviii. 2, whose first year Africanus made his epoch for the Exodus.

Africanus gives 1797 for this epoch : he makes the Hebrews identical with the Hyksos, and reckons for the sojourning 215 years.

Josephus also identifies the Hebrews with the Hyksos so far as the expulsion date is concerned ; but dates the Exodus 1681, and makes the Hyksos supreme in Egypt 511 (or 518) years, from Salatis to Amosis, thus, as I suppose : Dyn. xv. 260 years ; xvi. 251 years ; expulsion war 7 years. But as he reckons 215 for the sojourn, he must have made the Eisode come under some king of his hypothetical Dyn. xvi. From this point he calculates thus :

Dyn. xviii.	267 years
And intercalates [60 years +] 66 for Ramses Miamun	126
Sum .	393
then he counts Seti 59 and R. ii. a second time, 66 .	125
and so gets his total ; Amosis to Mineptah . .	518

an artificial pendant to the 518 Salatis to Amosis.

Before discussing the details of the story of Amenofis, which Josephus quotes in full, let us see what the dates in Manetho (as I give them) actually are. The 26th year of Apofis (the traditional date of the Eisode) falls on 1752 B.C. ; from this date, taking 430 years for the sojourn, we get 1322 for the Exodus, which falls under Amenofath xviii. 15 in Africanus' list. This king, therefore, is, on Manetho's calculation, the Pharaoh of the Exodus : Mineptah is out of the question, as from 26th Apofis to the end of Ramessu ii. would, at the very least, be more than 507 years on any calculation, which is more than any chronologer, ancient or modern, will concede.

It becomes necessary, therefore, to examine the data for the last 25 years of Dyn. xviii. with great care. The monumental evidence is quite clear.

	Y.	M.
Horemheb reigned over 20 years, say, as a minimum . .	20	1
Ramessu i. reigned over 1 year alone, say, as Josephus gives	1	4
Ramessu i. with Seti i. as coadjutor to the end of xviii. .	3	6
Sum .	24	11

This gives Ramessu i. a reign of nearly 5 years in all : but is it possible to reconcile these numbers with the lists ? With our present texts it is not possible ; we must have recourse to conjecture. For the first item I would read ∩∩ (20) in place of IIII (4) in Josephus' number : and I suppose that this mistake having omitted 16 years, the same amount was added to 3 in the last item to restore the true sum. The second item is doubtless correct.

With these corrected numbers let us consider the story of Amenofis, as given by Josephus from Manetho.

A King Amenofis (which name, he says, was not his true one, but assumed) of uncertain date wanted to see the gods as his predecessor, Horus, had done; therefore he applied to Amenofis, son of Paapis the priest, who gave the king his name and told him he might see the gods, if he would expel all lepers from the land. He collected the lepers (80,000) and sent them to work in quarries east of the Nile, among them certain learned priests: the priest Amenofis then, fearing the wrath of the gods, warned the king by letter that there were those who would fight with them and rule Egypt for 13 years. Having written this, he killed himself. The king in despondency gave Avaris to the lepers. Osarsif, their leader, sent to the shepherds at Jerusalem for help; they send 200,000 men. The king does not fight them; but, leaving " his son Sethos, also called Ramses after his father," then 5 years old, retires to Ethiopia for 13 years. After this he returns with an army, and with his son Ramses, also with an army, drives the lepers to the borders of Syria.

Now this priest Amenofis, son of Paapis, is certainly the great architect, Amenhotep, son of Hapi, the royal scribe of Amenhotep iii. (Horus), who "found forms of mysteries for amulets"—*i.e.*, litanies of magic names. He was in high office in the 11th year of Amenhotep iii., 1406 B.C., and must, when consulted by the king, *c.* 1340, have been a very old man—nearly 90. This, however, is quite possible, and need not disparage Manetho's statement. The important inference from this part of the story is that the name which the king assumed for his inter-

E

view with the gods was, according to Josephus, the
same as the priest's, Amenhotep, and not Meneptah
or Merenptah. The modern identifications of this
King Amenofis with the 3rd king of Dyn. xix. are
therefore impossible. There can be hardly any doubt
that he is the same as the Amenofath of Africanus'
list, which, be it remembered, comes from the same
source as the story in Josephus: for if Amenofath is
not the Josephus Amenofis, he is not mentioned by
that author at all. The following scheme appears
to me to reconcile all the variant accounts of this
period:

B.C.
1342. Horemhib's accession.
1336. Ramessu i. "sees the gods," then goes to Ethiopia
      for 13 y.
1323–2. R. i. returns: Seti now 19 years of age.
1322. Exodus. Horemhib dies. R. i. reigns alone.
1321. Seti is associated in the government.
1318. The Sothic epoch of Menofres (Ramessu i.).
1317. Seti i. succeeds.

I have little doubt that the whole narrative is a
folk-lore tale: but all the Egyptian stories of this
kind appear to have been more accurate in their
historical backgrounds than is usually supposed.
Details are, therefore, worth consideration. The
name Amenofis in Josephus occurs 5 times, (1, 2) as
equivalent to Amenhotep i., ii.; (3) as (in the present
instance) equivalent to Menpehti; (4) as equivalent
to Meneptah; and (5) as equivalent to Amenhotep the
priest. These names are carefully discriminated in
the other lists.

	AFR.	EUS.	JOS.
1. Amenhotep	Amenofthis	Amofis	
2. Amenhotep	Amenofis	Amenofis	Amenofis
3. Menpehti	Amenofath	Omitted	
4. Merenptah	Ammenefthes	Amenefthis	

The name Amenofath is consequently not Amen-hotep, as Josephus thought, but Men·peh·ti; just as its other Greek transliteration Men·of·res is Men·-peh·ra, each being a form of the name of Ramessu i. mistakenly created by Manetho into a separate personage, as xiii. 3, Amenemhat Shotepabra is, in the Turin list, generally separated into two kings. From this separation of Ramessu i. into two kings arose the strange blunder of Josephus (it can hardly be Manetho's) that Seti was also called Ramses.

Another question requiring solution is, Whence did Josephus get his sum-numbers 393 and 518? He could scarcely have invented them. As to 393, Jose-phus reckons xviii. 14–18, 151 years, and xviii. 1–13, 242 years; Manetho's reckoning (after the corrup-tion of 20y. 1m. into 4y. 1m. for Armais) is xvii. 151 years, xviii. 1–14, 242 years. Josephus has shifted the epoch of the Hyksos' expulsion from the erroneous end-to-end position at the end of Dyn. xvi. to its right place at the beginning of xviii., and then, in order to get the 151 years (which he ought to have left out altogether) included somewhere in his scheme, has inserted a duplication of Ramses ii., and another forgery of 60 years at the end of xviii.

The 518 years, which in Manetho constitute the

total time of the Hyksos from Salatis to Osarsiph (Dyn. xvi.), are reckoned by Josephus as xv. 260 years + xvi. 251 years + 7 years' war, and he then repeats the number 518 thus: xviii. 393 years + xix. 1-2, 125 years. There was really only one such period—xv. 260 years + xviii. 1-16 (to the Exodus) 258 years; and the *terminus ad quem* was Menpehti Amenofath, not Mineptah Amenofis, as Josephus would have it.

If my view be the true one, the princess who adopted Moses—the Thermouthis of Josephus— must have been Mertaten (Merthouthis ?), daughter of Akhenaten: at the time of the Exodus Moses would be about 50 years old. The way in which Pithom is mentioned in Ex. i. 11 would imply that it was the earliest town of this name, and there is no reason for preferring the second to the first Ramses as the Pharaoh of oppression. The culmination of bondage seems to have been reached under Horem- hib while Ramessu i. was in Ethiopia. Manetho places the rule of the Hyksos under Osarsif (? Asar- siptah) at that time.

Connected with this time Josephus quotes another bit of folk-lore, telling how one of " the two brothers," Hermaios (or Armais) Danaos was left by the other, Sethos Aigyptos, in charge of the kingdom; how he misconducted himself and was dethroned on Sethos' return from his wars with Cyprus and Phœnicia, the Assyrians, and the Medes. Here again we have a historic background, for Hermaios can hardly be any other than Horemhib; and there is nothing alleged against the hypothesis of Brugsch, with whom

E. Meyer agrees, that Ramessu i. was brother to Horemhib. Moreover, R. i. is known to have been an old man at the time of his accession, which agrees with the hypothesis. R. i. did war with the Syrians, and most probably it was he who concluded the treaty with Sapalulu, King of the Khita. Every fact known of him is consistent with his having been a claimant of the crown before he was driven into Ethiopia in the 6th year of Horemhib, who was the Pharaoh, I suppose, of the Exodus. No son of Horemhib's is known; but an infant son may have died not long before the Exodus, as we may infer from the Biblical narration.

The confusion of names in Josephus, who calls Hermaios' brother Sethos, and Seti i. Ramses "after his father," arises from his unwarranted interpolations. His list in this part must have been :

The brothers {	Armais Aigyptos	4, 1 years
	[Sethos *a*	60, 0]
	Ramesses *a*	1, 4
	Armesses *b*	66, 2
	Amenofis *a*	19, 6
	Sethosis *b*	59, 0
	Rampses *c*	66, 0
J.'s Pharoah of Exode	Amenofis *b*	?
	Sethos *c*	

Josephus has inserted his supposititious Sethos *a* in the place that Ramessu i. ought to occupy : hence his first mistake making Sethos, not Ramses, brother of Armais ; and he has taken Sethos *c* (Seti ii.) to be the son of the Exode Pharoah Amenofis *b* (Mer-enptah) instead of Sethos *b* (Seti i.), son of Amenofis *a* (Ramses i.), the real expeller of the lepers ;

hence his second mistake. The tell-tale phrase is "named after his father Ramses." The father of Seti ii. was not a Ramses; the father of Seti i. was. The moderns, the majority of whom adopt Josephus' erroneous hypothesis, interpolate "grand" in the text, and read "after his grandfather." They also (being unaware or oblivious of the certain fact that Josephus, Africanus, Eusebius, and most Christian* chronologers until Michaelis, reckoned the 430 years of Ex. xii. 40 from the call of Abram and the sojourning in Egypt as only 215 years) assert that the attribution of the Eisode to the 26th of Apofis is the calculation of some Alexandrian Jew, who obtained it by calculating 430 years back from Aahmes to Apofis. This is utterly wrong : no known Jew calculated 430 years for the sojourn : nor can the number 430 be got at from Aahmes in any numbers in Manetho. The only ancient authorities who ascribe a sojourn of this amount are the author of Ex. xii. and Manetho himself : and his 430 years expire in the reign of Amenofath—*i.e.*, of Ramessu i. For my part, I hold that they are right, and that the Exode took place 1322 B.C., only 10 years from 1312, the date assigned by the modern Jews, and agreeing in the main with that of Lepsius. The only note of time of any importance in the Biblical Hebrew chronology that does not agree with my Egyptian scheme is the 480 years of 1 Kings, vi. 1.

* The exceptions are Clemens of Alexandria and Theophilus of Antioch.

MANETHO'S THIRD VOLUME.

From the end of Manetho's twenty-first dynasty we stand on historical ground; the contemporary Hebrew monarchs from Rehoboam onwards affording definite dates for comparison; and later on the history of Persia also giving means of correction in various cases of doubt. Moreover, the stelæ of the Apis bulls and the genealogies of the Egyptian architects provide abundant tests of the correctness of the chronological data obtained by these other means. All this period has been examined by skilled hands, and I should have omitted it altogether, were it not that the "totals" in Manetho's system and in that of the Old Chronicle necessitate a statement of the regnal years and kings of these later dynasties. But I must ask the reader to bear in mind that my first object is not to fix the true chronology but to determine what was the system actually received by the Egyptian priests : and that however I may judge (as I have doubtless indicated more often than I am aware of) that this was a true system back as far as 2000 B.C. at least, still that this is a separate question, not the main aim of the present treatise.

DYNASTY XX. (DIOSPOLITE.)

This dynasty consisted of 12 kings, 135 years (Afr.), 172 years (Eus.). Eusebius evidently included Ramses iii., and many modern writers even include Setnekht in direct opposition to Manetho, and solely from their own conclusion that he ought to be made the founder of a new line. My own opinion is that Manetho was right, and that he opened his new dynasty at the point where Ramses iii. began to be contemporary with Dynasty xxi. It seems impossible in any other way to get the date 1207 B.C. for the accession of Merenptah xix. 3. But this date, founded on Mahler's astronomical data, is one of the most certainly established that we possess, and is admitted even by Professor Petrie. The 12 kings, whoever they were, were certainly the last 9 Ramses, *i.e.*, Ramses iv.-xii. in my reckoning, and 3 others.

The only succession list is that of the Sothis book, but this in this instance agrees closely with the monuments.

Kings.			Years.	Sothis.	Years.	Adopted.	B.C.
1. Ra. iv.	heqma		11+	Psammouthis	13	16	1108
2. „ v.	skheperen		4+				
3. „ vi.	nebma		—				
4. „ vii.	atamen		—		4	4	1092
5. „ viii.	khunamen		—				
6. „ ix.	skhanra		—	Kertos	20	1	1088
7. „ x.	neferkara		19+			19	1087
8. „ xi.	khamuas		27+	Rampses	45	27	1068
9. „ xii.	khepermara		—				
10. { Saamen (co-regent) =						18	1041
{ Herhor (alone)		See				6	1023
11. Pinezem i.		Dyn.				9	1017
12. Pisebkhan i.		xxi.				35	1008
						135	

The abbreviated names are merely given to identify the
Ramessus clearly.

It would be useless to re-investigate the order of these Ramessus after the masterly exposition of Mr. Cecil Torr, from whose work I have frequently obtained corrections of detail. I need not say that I differ in the conclusions to be drawn from the data, but as a statement of the data his book seems to me unrivalled.

I accept the old conjecture that Osokhor, Psinakhes and Psousennes are identical with Herhor, Pinezem and Pisebkhan, as thereby perfect clearness and consistency are introduced into this confused period; but I do not deny that xx. 10–12 may have been obscure Ramessus, at present unidentified, contemporary with these 3 kings.

The sums of Eusebius for Dyn. xix., xx., 162 + 172, compared with 209 + 135 of Africanus, indicate that he included Ramessu iii., with a reign of 37 years in Dyn. xx. As to his stated sum 194 years for xix., it is merely the 194 of the Chronicler for Dyn. xviii., stolen and put in the wrong place.

See further under Dyn. xxi.

DYNASTY XXᴀ.

That a dynasty of 143 years has been omitted from the lists of Manetho and Africanus I deduce elsewhere from the total of Manetho's third volume and from Africanus' date for the Exodus. No trace of such a dynasty in detail is to be found in any list except the Mestræan, where we find

59. Athothis = Fousanos	28 years	
60. Kenkenes	39	
61. Ouenefes	42	
62. Sousakeim	34	
Sum	143	

I have no doubt this is the dynasty in question, but where was it meant to be placed chronologically? Athothis is distinctly identified with Fousanos, in whose time the first earthquake took place in Egypt. This must have been the earthquake that overthrew the temple at Tanis, which Sa Amen of Dyn. xxi. found in ruins. This would make Athothis come between Ramessu iii. and Sa Amen, and therefore I put Dyn. xxʌ. in this place. But it is entirely un-historical: 3 kings are taken, names, dates, and all, from Dyn. i. 2–4, and the fourth (Sheshonk) xxii. 1 is quite out of place. The Redactor invented this dynasty to make up his mystical 3650 years from Horus to Ptolemy III., and although Africanus had it in his first list, he was quite right in rejecting it in his final revision.

DYN. XXI.—(*See Table facing this page.*)

Psousennes, 14 ∩IIII should read ∩∩∩ 30: in all else Africanus is, I think, right. Eusebius possibly got his 35 years from the Dyn. xx. reckoning, and altered the other Psousennes from 46 to 41 to set his sum right. The Sothis book list is of no utility here, but interesting as showing how numbers were invented by this chronographer. The 50 for Thouosis is made up of the true number 46 and the consecutive 4 for Psousennes, and in like manner the 15 for

DYNASTY XXI. (TANITE.)

MONUMENTS.	ADOPTED.	AFRICANUS.	YEARS.	EGS.	SOTHIS.	YEARS.	B.C.
1. Nisi Batattat	26	Smendes'	26	26	57. Amendes	27	1108
2. Pisebkhan i.	46	Psousennes	46	41	58. Thouoris	50	1082
3. Nuterkara	4	Nefelkheres	4	4	65. Nefekheres	6	1036
4. Amenemapt	9	Amenofthis	9	9	64. Amenofis	9	1032
5. Hirhor	6	Osorkhon	6	6	66. Saites	15	1023
6. Pinezem i.	9	Psinakhes	9	9	67. Psinakhes	9	1017
7. Pisebkhan ii.	29	Psousennes	14	35	63. Psousennes	25	1008
Sums	120		114	130		141	979
Sum stated	—		130	130		—	—

[To face page 74.

Saites = Sa-Amen = Hirhor of the true 6 and consecutive 9. The most important help to chronology
is obtained from the mummies at Deir el Bahri. I
give here dates only, as all other needful particulars
are so easily accessible in Petrie, ii. 337.

Kings with Regnal Years.			B.C.	Superintending Priests.
xx. 7	Ramessu x.	16	1073	Amenhotep
xx. 8	[Ramessu xi.]	6	1063	Hirhor
				Piankhi
,,	[,,]	17	1052	Pinezem i.
	Saamen	6	1051	,,
	,,	13	1044	,,
				Zet Khensuafankh
	,,	16	1041	Masahart
	,,	25	1032	Pasebkhanu ii.
xxi. 4	Amenemapt	6	1026	,,
xxi. 1	,,	20	1023	Pinezem ii.
xxi. 5	Hirhor			,,
xxi. 6	Pinezem i.			,,
xxi. 7	Pasebkhanu ii.	9	1000	,,
,,	,,	16	993	,,
,,	,,			Shashank xxii. 1
,,	,,			Auaput xxii. 2

The insertion of Ramessu xi. is conjectural, no
name being endorsed on the mummies in these instances. Petrie says the king was Pasebkhanu i.
and that the name was endorsed, but gives no
evidence or reference to any authority. Hirhor is
known elsewhere as priest to Ramessu xi., but as
priest to Pasebkhanu I have searched for him in
vain.

Saamen, from the way in which he is inserted
between Pasebkhanu and Amenemapt, seems to be
regarded by Petrie as a king of Dyn. xxi., and
he expressly states on very inconclusive grounds

that he is not to be identified with Herhor.   I
take him to be the same as Herhor and place
him in Dyn. xx. immediately after Ramessu xii.,
but although I think this view far more probable
than Petrie's, I do not say that his is impossible:
in either case it is a tight fit, not too tight, however, to get room for Saamen at all.   If Petrie
is right, he must have been co-regent with Pasebkhanu i. for 21 years and with Nuterkara for 6.
If I am right, he was co-regent with Ramessu xi.
(from his 18th year onward) and with Ramessu xii.
whom he succeeded as sole ruler, uniting the rival
dynasties xx. of Thebes and xxi. of Tanis.   On the
hypothesis that xx. and xxi. were contemporary all
is clear: if xxi. succeeded xx. no scheme that I have
seen is even possible.

The working careers of this family were long.
Herhor was priest in 1063, died 1017 (46 years);
Painezem held office from 1052 to 1009 (43 years);
and Pasebkhanu from 1032 to 979 (53 years) at
least.

Dyn. XXII.—(See Table facing this page.)

Eusebius and the Sothis give only 1, 2, 6: 49
years.   I adopt for the order of the kings Cecil
Torr's conclusive statement.   The Chronicler follows
some contemporaneous line—perhaps Usarkon Miamun, who was king of Bubastis, while Pamaa and
Shashank iii. were only satraps, as we know from
the account of Piankhi's invasion.   In this case
Usarkon would be a rival king to Takelot ii. for
6 years, seeing that the Chronicler splits his dynasty

DYNASTY XXII. (BUBASTITE.)

MONUMENTS.		YEARS.	AFRICANUS.	YEARS.	ADOPTED.	B.C.
1 Shashank i.	Hezkheperra	21 +	1. Sesonkhis	21	31	979
2 Auaput	son of Shashank	?				
3 Usarkon i.	Usermara	23 +	2. Osorkhon	15	25	948
4 Takelot i.	Usermara	23 +	3-5.	25	25	923
5 Shashank ii.	Usermara	29 +			30	898
6 Takelot ii.	Hezkheperra	15			15	868
7 Usarkon ii.	Kherpkheperra	?	6. Takelothis	13		
8 Pamaa	Usermara	2 +	7-9.	42	42	653
9 Shashank iii.	Aakheperra	37 +				
Sums		150 +	Sum stated	116	168	811
				120		

[To face page 76.

into two of 121 and 48 years respectively. This is, however, mere guess: the important point is his total 169 years. Africanus' 116 or 120 must be wrong: the monuments give 30 years more than this. It seems to me that the original authority for Africanus' list was compiled from a partially defaced monument in which some of the tens were obliterated. I would therefore restore 31, 25, 55 for his first three numbers—21, 15, 25.

There was a Sed feast in the 22nd year of Usarkon Usermara. If my arrangement is right this ought to come at an interval of $28x$ from 1318 B.C. Now 22 Usarkon $= 926$ and $1318 - 926 = 392 = 14 \times 28$. This important test is therefore satisfied.

Manetho's original numbers are conjecturally restored in " Schemes " further on : the Redactor's were perhaps the same as those which I have adopted.

I admit the identity of Menkheperra and Paseb-khanu ii. (see Cecil Torr's admirably clear statement of the reasons), and I believe that for Nefelkheres in Africanus we ought to read Netherkeres.

Since writing the above I have read Maspero's new arrangement (*Histoire Ancienne*, ii. 762). He places Saamen after Amenemapt, which necessitates Menkheperra coming before Masahart in the midst of the priesthood of Painezem i. ; but suppresses all the inconsistent details.

I cannot in any way admit that Egyptologists are justified in inserting another Usarkon as some do, or in cutting down this dynasty in opposition to the Egyptian chroniclers by making the Sheshonk

of Piankhi's inscription to be Usermara as others
do.   If this Sheshonk be Aakheperra perfect coincidence with the Old Chronicle is obtained, and, as in
every other instance from Dyn. xviii. onward he has
proved a safe guide, I cannot reject his leading in
this case.   Brugsch seems to me to have been
misled by assuming that the descendants of the
same grade in two contemporary lines must also
be contemporary—a most unsound rule, especially
in Oriental families, where elderly monarchs were
so habitually married to young brides.   I may
quote a striking instance of this in the Assyrian
King Burnaburyas: and in this very dynasty we
find in Brugsch six high priests—Pinotem ii.,
Anupoth, Sheshonk, Nimrod, Osarkon, Sheshonk,
which gives a fair average of 28 years to a generation; alongside of nine architects—Horemsaf i.,
Mermer, Horemsaf ii., Zahib i., Nasshunu i., Zahib ii.,
Nasshunu ii., Zahib iii., and Nasshunu iii.   Brugsch
is compelled on his principle to give these men a
period of 300 years. Of course from my point of view,
until we attain precise knowledge of what kings
were contemporary with each of these men, the only
use that can be made of this genealogy is to test the
total number of years during dynasties xxi.–xxvi.,
and we must abstain from the sweeping conclusion
of the learned and ingenious author, who builds so
much of his system on generations of 33 years.

DYNASTY XXIII. (TANITE.)

AFRICANUS.	YEARS.	EUSEBIUS.	MONUMENTS.	B.C.
1. Petubastes	40	25	Petsibast	811
2. Osorkho	8	9	Osorkhon	771
3. Psammus	10	10	Psimut	763
4. Zet	31	—		753
Total	89	44		722

I have no doubt that Manetho had good authority for his numbers, and that Africanus has faithfully reproduced them : but the historical difficulties are considerable, and the genealogies do not make matters clear. Moreover, there must have been at this time rival dynasties in different parts of Egypt, for at this period the Chronicler gives a dynasty of Diospolites, 2 kings who reigned 19 years ; and he does not again coincide with Manetho till the twenty-sixth Dynasty —the Persians. In all probability the course of future discovery will confirm this most trustworthy authority. Meanwhile we can only wait and hope.

DYNASTY XXIV. (SAITE.)

1. Bokkhoris, 6 years (Africanus), 722-716 B.C.

Eusebius says 44 years ; but he has, as is customary with him, taken this number from the Old Chronicle and given it an erroneous interpretation. This king is doubtless Bokenranf whose Apis sarcophagus was deposited in the same chamber as that of the Apis deceased in the 37th year of Shashank iv. But so far from this " bringing to light a connexion in time " between these monarchs, as Brugsch tells us, it absolutely disproves their contemporaneity; for had they been contemporaneous and therefore rival kings, they would not both have had access to the Serapeum. A careful analysis shows that many contemporaneities assumed by Brugsch in the body of his work are contradicted by the table of kings placed at the end thereof.

DYNASTY XXV. (ETHIOPIAN.)

	AFR.	EUS.	MONUMENTS.	B.C.
1. Sabakon	8	12	Shabak	716
2. Sebikhos	14	12	Shabatak	708
3. Tarakos	18	20	Taharaka, 27	694
Sum	40	44		686

The dates of Eusebius are again manifestly taken from the Old Chronicle. Now at last we get a definite connexion with Assyrian history and from this point every date can be fixed with as great a certainty as can be obtained for any ancient history whatever.

But an important difficulty remains to be solved. Taharaka (Tarakos) immediately preceded Psamtik i. of Dynasty xxv. in the Memphite reckoning, for an Apis-stele expressly states that an Apis born in the 26th year of Taharaka died aged 21 in the 20th year of Psamtik i., Taharaka therefore reigned 27 years. Either he or Tefnakht, Nekhepso and Nekho in the next dynasty must have been absent from the original list of Manetho. Modern Egyptologists omit the three kings : but this entirely disorganises Africanus' list for the next dynasty by necessitating an alteration of the numbers both of kings and years : it also leaves the numbers in the Old Chronicle unexplained. But if we replace the 18 years of Taharaka by 8 everything falls into clear order. Further examination is therefore required. Now consider the following table which contains the name of every king mentioned in the lists or the monuments from Petsibast to Psamtik.

B.C.	TANITES.	SAITES.	FROM ETHIOPIA.	KUSHITES.
580	Setise xxiii.	Tafnakht	M. Piankhi (xxiii.)	
811	1. Petsibast 40	? (xxiv.)	(1) Mia. Nut) 19 (2) Piankhi }	Kashta
792		(1) } 44		
771	2. Usarkon 8	(2) }		
763	3. Psimut 10	(3) }		
753	4. Zet 31		(xxv.)	
748		xxiv. [16]	(1) Kashta [26]	Rudamon i.
722		1. Bokenranf 6	(2) } xxv. {(14)	
716			1. } Shabak { 8	
708	(xxvi.)	[Amyrtaios 4]	2. } Shabatak {14	{ Aqel's husband
704	(1). Sethon [37]		(3) } {(4)	{ Ammeres 18
694		xxvi.		3. Taharaka 27
686		1. Setepennit 7		
679		2. Nekhepso 6		
673		3. Nekho 6		
667	Dodekarkhy 15	4. Psamtik 54		Rudamon ii.

Africanus, or rather Manetho, reckons thus: 4 Tanites : Petsibast, Usarkon, Psimut, Zet; 1 Saite : Bokenranf; 3 Ethiopians : Shabak, Shabatak, Taharaka; 9 Saites : Setepennit, Nekhepso, Nekho, Psamtik, &c. His only error is in the years of Taharaka, which should be 8 instead of 18, the years

F

of xxvi., 1–3, being contemporaneous with the last
19 years of his reign. This is compensated by the
omission of 10 years in xxvi., 5. The Chronicler
has 2 Diospolites (who must have been Miamun Nut
and Piankhi), 19 years ; 3 Saites (the missing
generations between Tafnakht and Bokenranf), 44
years; 3 Ethiopians, Kashta (or possibly Rudamon i.),
Shabak and Shabatak (this last for 4 years only to
the accession of Sethon), 44 years ; and finally 7
Memphites for 177 years. As 6 kings and 140 years
are already provided from Psamtik onwards, this
requires 1 king and 37 years just before Psamtik ;
I would identify this king with the Herodotean
Sethon, who may or may not be the same as Ammeres
the Ethiopian, whose epoch is identical. Ammeres
was, I doubt not, the husband of Aqel, who was
daughter of Rudamon i.

It appears then that so far from Manetho and the
Chronicler being at utter variance, these two accounts
are strictly supplementary ; one giving us the succession received as legitimate by the Memphite priests,
and therefore in strict accordance with the Apis-
stelæ ; the other giving the succession according to the
priests of Heliopolis. The more minutely their details
are analysed, the more trustworthy do the native
historians prove to be. In this case the whole foundation of the discredit involved in their supposed
contradictions has arisen from a transposition of
10 years.

Slight discrepancies in dates (never more than two
years) will be noted by the careful reader : these
arise from a difference of reckoning between Manetho

and the Chronicle : I am compelled to follow Manetho, as his list alone gives full details of the succession ; but have no doubt the Chronicle will ultimately prove to be correct.

With regard to Psamtik i. I must add a few lines in order to traverse a possible objection, that I make him far too late, for was he not husband to Shepenapet, the daughter of King Piankhi and Ameniritis ? True it is that he is so represented in the genealogical table in Brugsch ("Egypt under the Pharaohs," Eng. trans. ii. 190) ; but on reference to the text of the same work, ii. 272, we find that Shepenapet was not daughter, but great-great-granddaughter of Ameniritis. This exactly agrees with my results, and at the same time shows that the whole latter part of Brugsch's table is erroneous for 8 generations at least. Nothing is more misleading than genealogy, which has to be pieced up from miscellaneous items, if the same names recur at intervals as they do in these families.

The discrepancies in Eusebius arise from his having adopted the year-sums of the Chronicler for Dyn. xxiv. and xxv. without in the least understanding them : he may, however, be right in giving 6 years to xxvi. 3, Nekhoa (which would require 8 years for the portion of Taharaka's reign before Tafnakht), and we owe to him the mention of Ammeres. The only other authority needing consideration is Herodotus, and I confess that to me the accuracy of this author in reporting his authorities appears to have been attacked inconsiderately and unfairly. He gives :

1. Anysis of Anysis, the blind king.
2. Sabako the Ethiopian, 50 years.
3. Blind king again ; but now apparently under the name of Amyrtaios.
4. Sethon, the priest of Hefaistos (Ptah).
5. Dodekarkhy (included in Psamtik by Manetho).
6. Psamtik.

The only inaccuracies appear to be (1) the name of the blind king; (2) the 50 years of Sabako. As to the years I believe that, although the text of Herodotus, wherein this number is repeated at least three times, cannot well be corrupt, still he may easily have mistaken his original note of 8 years (H) for 50 (N), and 8 is the true number: as to Anysis I suggest that Amyrtaios is the true reading, the name of the town having been repeated by mistake; in which case Amyrtaios may be identical with Bokenranf, who was burned by Sabako the Second, Amyrtaios being a pretender of the stamp of Perkin Warbeck or the false Demetrius. Of the real existence of Sethon I see no reason to doubt. He was probably a Memphite, being a priest of Ptah, though placed for convenience of printing in the Tanite column in my table. The regnal years in brackets are obtained by calculation and inserted by myself. With the arrangement thus made I can discover no inconsistency : others may be successful in doing so. The invasion of Sennakherib (700 B.C.) falls, as it should, in Sethon's time, and the data of the Apis-stelæ are satisfactorily accounted for. One thing seems to me certain : Sethon was not Sabako. That Bokkhoris was the same as Amyrtaios is much more probable : and it is worth mention

DYNASTY XXVI. (SAÏTE.)

	AFR.	EUS.	MONUMENTS.	HERODOTUS.		ADOPTED.	B.C.
0. Ammeres Æthiops	—	18	Tafnakht				686
1. Stefinates	7	7	Nekhepso				679
2. Nekhepsos	6	6	Neku i.	Dodekarkhy			673
3. Nekhoa	8	6	Psamtik i.				667
4. Psammitikhos	54	44	Neku ii.	Psammitikhos	54	54	667
5. Nekhoa ii.	6	6	Psamtik ii.	Neko	16	16	613
6. Psammuthis	6	17	Uahabra	Psammis	6	6	597
7. Vafris (Apries)	19	25	Aahmes	Apries	25	19	591
8. Amosis	44	42	—	Amosis	44	44	572
9. Psammekherites	0, 6 m	—		Psammenites	0, 6	1	528
Sum	150, 6 m	171			145, 6	140	527

[To face page 95.

that a cartoon at Sais, at first supposed to contain the name of Amyrtaios (Dyn. xxviii.), who also reigned 6 years, was afterwards found to relate to Bokkhoris.

The reign of Bokenranf is known from the monuments as 16 years at the least, 10 of which must have been contemporary with Zet = Kashta, whom Manetho prefers to acknowledge as legitimate.

DYN. XXVI.—(*See Table facing this page.*)

The only error of any import in Africanus is his assigning only 6 years instead of 16 to Nekhoa ii. Eusebius has corrected the wrong 6 and given Psammetichus 10 years in excess; he has also several other mistakes. His insertion of Ammeres is, as we have seen, of some importance; but is not taken from Manetho; in this later history there is no other instance from Dyn. xxii. onwards of Manetho's registering contemporaneous kings. I am fully aware that in making this assertion I am exposing myself to an attack from certain Egyptologists, who will allege the genealogies against me. But I believe the evidence of Manetho, and also that the moderns have been misled : (1) by mistaking Shashank Usermara for Shashank Aakheperra as the contemporary of Miamun Piankhi; (2) by confusing Tafnakht, the father or ancestor of Bokenranf, with Tafnakht the father of Nekhepso; (3) by confusing Miamun Piankhi with Piankhi, father of Kashta.

DYNASTY XXVII. (PERSIAN.)

Monuments.	Africanus.	Years.	Eus.	B.C.
1. Kambathat	Kambyses	6	3	527
2. Ntariush	Darius Hystaspas	36	36	521
3. Khsharish	Xerxes	21	21	485
4. Khabbash	Artabanus	0, 7 m	0, 7m	464
5. Artakhsharisha	Artaxerxes	41	40	463
6.	Xerxes	0, 2	0, 2	
7.	Sogdianus	0, 7	0, 7	
8. Ntariush	Darius	19	19	423
		124, 4 m	120, 4m	

The Chronicle has 5 Persians, 124 years.

Eusebius alone has numbers that agree with history and with the data which will be found in the final review of Manetho's system : the error of 4 years in the sum given, 124 years, appears to have originally crept in from the 4 months.

DYNASTY XXVIII. (SAITE.)

1. Armenartrut Amyrtaios, 6 years. B.C. 403.

DYNASTY XXIX. (MENDESIAN.)

Monuments.	Africanus.	Years.	Eus.	Adopted.	B.C.
1. Nefaarut	Neferites	6	6	6	397
2. Hakori	Akhoris	13	13	13	391
3. Psimut	Psammouthis	1	1	1	378
4. Nefaarut	Neferites	0, 4	0, 4	0, 4	
5. Hornebka	Memthis	—	1	1	377
		20, 4	21, 4	21, 4	

DYNASTY XXX. (SEBENNYTE.)

MONUMENTS.	AFRICANUS.	YEARS.	EUS.	ADOPTED.	B.C.
1. Nakhtherhib	Nektanebos	18	10	16	376
2. Zihu	Teos	2	2	2	360
3. Nekhtnebef	Nektanebos	18	8	18	358
		38	20	36	340

In place of these two latter dynasties the Chronicle has :
>   xxix. 39 years.
>   xxx. 1 Tanite, 18 years, *i.e.*, Nektanebos ii.

The discussion of these later dynasties—xxvii.–xxx.—would be very lengthy and make the book considerably larger than would be desirable at present : the two or three years in doubt not in any way affecting my main thesis.

ON THE APIS-STELÆ.

With regard to the Apis-stelæ found by Mariette in the Serapeum, it may be convenient, as I have had several times to refer to them, to sum up very briefly their contents, so as to show the amount of help for chronological investigation hitherto derived from them.

It is probable that the "step-pyramid" of Sakkara was the Kakami or black-bull pyramid built by Uenephes as a common sepulchre for the Apis bulls. It would seem that before 1580 the Serapeum was fashioned to replace this pyramid. The date is, I think, fixed by the statement (if we can trust it) appended to the name Aseth, the last of the six shepherd kings. "In his time the heifer was deified and called Apis": this cannot, of course, refer to the recognition of Apis as a divinity; that had been done under Kakau in the very earliest time; it must indicate some special public recognition of the deification: no such recognition is known unless it be the establishment of the Serapeum and the erection therein of the Apis-stelæ, with the records of birth, "introduction," and death of each particular Apis.

If I am wrong in placing this event so early, at any rate 5 stelæ are extant of somewhat late reigns of Dynasty xviii., viz., of Amenhotep iii., Tutankh-Amen, Rathothis, and Horemhib. There are also 9 stelæ of Dynasty xix., under Seti i., Ramses ii., &c., and 9 more of Dynasty xx., under other Ramessus from iii. to xiv. All these are useful for confirmation of previously attained chronological results; but we do not gain from them any fresh information. But the contemporaneity of Dynasties xx. and xxi., which is one of the most peculiar features of the system advocated in the present book, is strongly confirmed by the fact that no Apis-stele has been discovered which belongs to either of the two Tanite dynasties xxi. or xxiii., or to the Mendesian xxix., although they have been found for every other dynasty down to the end of the history except the few doubtful years of xxviii. (Amyrtaios). This is very important: it shows that under Dynasty xxi. Memphis was still in the possession of the Ramessus, and that even under Dynasty xxiii. it was either held by their descendants, who had settled in Æthiopia; or else that Apis worship had fallen into abeyance. This latter supposition is most unlikely; and I have little doubt that the trustworthy Old Chronicler will prove to be right in calling his Dynasty xxiii. Diospolite; that they held Memphis; and that certain stelæ, which have been assigned to Dynasty xxi. by pure guess, will ultimately prove to belong to these Diospolites.

The 7 stelæ from Dynasty xxii. onward are far more useful. Besides giving us minimum numbers of regnal years—23 for Usarkon's; 13 for Takloth ii.; 36 for Shashank iv.—there is a series of inscriptions relating to an Apis, from which we gather that he was born in 28 Sheshenk iii., introduced into the temple on 1 Paophi, 28–9 of the same king, and buried 1 Mechir, 2 Pimai, aged 26 years. It is this inscription that absolutely fixes the relative dates of these three kings, necessitates their insertion (contrary to some modern Egyptologers) in the canon of succession, and vindicates the system of Manetho, who continues this dynasty down to Shashank. As a minor matter, I may note that the statement in one of these inscriptions that this Apis inauguration took place in the 28th year of Shashank iii., and in another that it was in the 29th, are not necessarily discrepant; rather I think do they show that the day of inauguration was the day on which the 28th year ended and the 29th began, the "coronation day," if I may so call it.

Again in Dynasty xxiv. we find a stele which proves that the 6 years assigned to Bokenranf by

Manetho are correct : and in Dyn. xxv. stelæ under the reigns of Shabak and Taharaka, and in Dyn. xxvi. a still more important one of an Apis born in the 26th year of Taharaka, inaugurated 9th Pharmuthi, died 20th Mesore in the 20th year of Psamtik i., and buried 25th Paophi, in the 21st year of the same king.   I have already utilised these stelæ in the determination of the regnal dates, but I may here point out that it is evident that Manetho did not entirely adopt the reckoning of either the Memphite priests or any other, so far as the legitimacy of succession is concerned. For instance he includes the Tanite dynasties in preference to the later Ramessus on the one hand, and Bokenranf, Shabak, and Shabatak in pre- ference to the " Kings of Kush " on the other.   But the Memphite priests certainly recognised the Saite and Diospolite dynasties, but not the Tanite or the Kings of Kush, with the one exception of Taharaka, who must have held possession of the town of Memphis.

The omission of Manetho to state any dynasties contemporary with xxii.–xxx. has been strongly urged as an argument against any contemporaneity among Dyn. vii.–xvii.: but the learned authorities who thus argue have overlooked the fact that the Turin papyrus (to say nothing of other schemes probably once existing) had already given details of every pre-Hyksos dynasty ; and Manetho was therefore bound to notice all these : whereas for the later time no list anterior to Manetho has come down to us which hints at more than a single line

of succession. For this time each author gave that
which seemed to him to be legitimate, and that
alone.

Returning to the Apis-stelæ, there are 4 others
under Dynasty xxvi., from which we obtain
minimum reigns of 52 years for Psamtik i., 16 for
Neku ii., 1 for Psamtik ii., 12 for Uahabra, and 5
for Aahmes. There are also stelæ dated under
Dynasties xxvii. and xxx. Had the series been
complete and unmutilated they would have supplied
an accurate chronological canon for all the period
from Dynasty xix. onward : but be it remembered only for those kings who held Memphis;
their rivals would still have had to be accounted for
in some other way. Even from the shattered stelæ
still extant considerable information has been
gleaned.

SECTION II.

THE MYTHIC DYNASTIES.

ALL the Egyptian schemes agree in considering
Menes as the first mortal king of their country ; but
anterior to him they place a series of gods and demigods, which varies according to the college of priests
who contrived it. The first divine king of the
Memphite scheme was Ptah; of the Heliopolite, Ra; of
the Hermonthite, Mentu ; of the Hermopolite, Thot ;
the Theban, Amen Ra. There is no direct evidence;

that Osiris was ever placed in this position, but Harsiesis was so reckoned in Ptolemaic times. This list is probably incomplete : Min, Anhur, Harsiesis, Sebek headed local Enneads just as those already enumerated, and may have had their local advocates for primal kingship. But only 3 of these schemes have come down to us as connected with the chronology—(1) the Memphite or Manethonic; (2) the Heliopolite or Chronicle ; (3) the scheme represented by the Turin papyrus. Of these the Memphite is the most complete.

MEMPHITE SCHEME.—(*See Table facing this page.*)

Every numeral in this table except those in square brackets in the "years" column is given on monumental authority. An examination of the parallel versions of demi-gods 7–10 shows that the original numbers are those given in Manetho (the small year numbers), and that these were subsequently enlarged first to seasons (*i.e.*, intervals from equinox to solstice, or conversely, not Egyptian "seasons") and then to months, each of the resulting numbers being counted as a year. The reverse process—that of a gradual diminution of the gods' reigns—cannot be entertained for a moment. This was recognised by the ancient chronologers, as is shown by the attempt of the editor of Manetho in Synkellos, who having only the larger month numbers before him for gods 1–6, has rightly reduced them to year numbers. Unfortunately he has mistaken the kind of month used by the priests ; the numbers of demi-gods 7-10 show that it should

MEMPHITE SCHEME.

[To face page 72.

Eg. Name.	Greek.	Gods.	ROUND. Months.	Months.	EXACT. L.NAR.	Years.	B.C.	? ORIGINAL.
1. Ptah	Hephaistos		9000	9000	734	730	2774	750
2. Ra	Helios		1000	992	80	82	2024	85
3. Shu	Agathodaimon		700	700	56	56	1941	28
4. Seb	Kronos		500	501	40	42	1862	42
5. Asar	Osiris		450	433	35	36	1810	36
6. Set	Tyfon		350	358	29	29	1804	30
		Sam	12000	11985	962 y. 8 m.	999 y.		1000
		Demi-gods.	Months.	Months.	Seasons.	Years.		
7. Haroeris?	Horos		300	304	100	25	1774	
8. Anhur	Ares		280	276	92	23	1749	
9. Anpu	Anubis		290	291	68	17	1726	
10. Harkaru	Herakles		180	190	60	15	1708	
		Sam	960	960	320	80		
			Seasons.	Months.	Seasons.	Years.		
11. Haroeris?	Apollo		100	304	104	25	1801	
12. Min?	Ammon		120	276	92	30	1629	
13. Tahuti	Tithoes		100	291	108	27	1623	
14. Sebek	Sonos		120	190	128	32	1612	
		Sam	440		156	114		
15. Amenra	Zeus		100		80	20	1590	92 6
16. Khons, &c.	4 others		370		370	30	1560	
20–29	30 D.G.				2650	[92 6]	1467	912 6
50–79	10 Thinites					350	555	350
							205	

be the twelfth part of the sacred year of 360 days, and for these kings he has the right numbers; but for the gods he has used lunar months of somewhat more than 29 days instead of 30, and so got his numbers here tabulated under "lunar." I have restored the true numbers between brackets. The total 11,985 is given by Manetho; but a variant reading is 11,988, which implies 504 years for Seb, which is a multiple of 12, and therefore probably correct. These different versions of the divine reigns were mixed up in later times so as to get Sothic epochs suiting the schemes of chronologers, as we shall see when I treat of these various systems. The following numerical relations are worth notice:

The years of the round total $12,000 + 960 + 440 + 100 + 370 = 13,870$: 19 semi-Sothic periods for 19 kings.

The 30 demi-gods (20–49) reign 30 Sothic months between them.

The difference for 19 kings between the round and exact reckonings is exactly 19 years: the average exact reign being 729 years: 729 is the cube of 9, but I do not find that this has any special significance. The demi-gods are arranged in groups of 4, in which the sum of the 1st and 4th = the sum of the 2nd and 3rd. This being true for every variant scheme must have been part of the original arrangement. Horus was therefore originally a demi-god, not one of the great gods as he appears in most late versions of the schemes.

These and other numerical relations will be

helpful by-and-by in explaining the manner in which the ancients concocted their mystical dates for Menes; but they do not explain how any scheme of divine reigns first originated. The usual explanation is that all these numbers were arbitrary inventions of the priests, but I do not believe in this sort of assumption. If we take the dates of the principal deities who we know were by the various chief priestly schools alleged to have been the first king of Egypt, viz., Ptah for Memphis, Ra for Heliopolis, Osiris for Bubastis (?), Thot for Hermopolis, and Amen Ra for Thebes, assuming as starting-point for Amen 1580 B.C. the epoch of Dyn. xviii., when Amen first became supreme all through the land, we shall find the following extraordinary coincidences :

B.C.	Epoch of	B.C.	Epoch of	
2778	Menes i.	2773	Ptah	Memphite
2024	Usertsen xii.	2023	Ra	Heliopolite
1840	Khyan xv.	1840	Osiris	Bubastite (?)
1630	Staan xv. 5	1639	Thoth	Hermopolite
1580	Aahmes xviii.	1580	Amenra	Theban

The years for the kings are those which I have shown (or tried to show?) in the whole of the preceding investigation to have been in use under Dyn. xviii., i.e., those of the Turin papyrus as it existed under Ramessu i. without the alteration made under Ramessu ii. See further on this under the head of Schemes. Even the one year's discrepancy between 2024 and 2023 may be avoided by adopting as the original version of the divine dynasty the integers in the last column of the scheme table instead of the fractions in brackets, and the introduction of Thot 9 years before the adoption of his Sed system (see under Seds) is not a discrepancy but an agreement.

It appears, then, that the intervals between the important changes of government by Dyn. i., xii., xv., xviii. are exactly the same as those assigned by the Memphite priests to Ptah, Ra, Osiris, Amen. I cannot believe this to be accidental. The divine dynasties are merely a replica of the political history of the country, setting forth the supremacy of the Memphite Ptah worshippers under i.–vi.; of the Ra worshippers of Heliopolis (probably as Mentu Ra of Hermonthis) under xii.; of the Osiris Delta-god under the Hyksos : and of Amenra under the Thebans of xviii. The scheme was probably made about 1560 B.C., as definite names cease at this point, and the after-dates 1467, 555, 205, do not point to any special epoch. If, however, Amen was included in the 4 others—and I cannot suppose that he stood as an odd man between two batches of 4 demi-gods each—these dates will become 1487, the very time when Hatshepsut and Thotmes iii. were introducing a changed Sed system and getting up their ancestral tree for Karnak ; 575, a very close date for Amosis, when the Saite priests were concocting their double Sothic from Menes; and 225, when Manetho's Redactor was forging his Ptolemaic system : all which remains for proof hereafter. I suppose the numbers in the " year " column to indicate the true

dates from a Memphite point of view of the successive introductions of the various deities into the
orthodox list. But these year numbers were not
those set forth publicly. The 6 great gods were
supposed to have reigns in which every month was
as good as an ordinary year, and therefore their
numbers were multiplied by 12; the 4 demi-gods
headed by Harsiesis were sometimes raised to the
same eminence, but sometimes dignified only by
having each season made equivalent to a year:
these 4 hovered between the reckoning assigned to
the great gods and that of the rest of the demigods who never attained the monthly reckoning, the
quarterly being their maximum in numeration, while
the very late addition of 10 Thinite kings and 350
years, which was not made till the demi-god list was
exhausted, are probably identical with the 10 Thinite
kings of Dyn. i., ii. and 351 years of Eratosthenes
(the Cynic cycle of the Chronicle): which stamps
these dynasties as partly mythic, although there
must be a historic basis for the existence of many
of their kings; the Sed cycles requiring a history
extending back to 2781 B.C. as a minimum date.
These various lists were mixed up and used indis-
criminately as suited the convenience of the chronologers.

My identification of the Greek names with
Egyptian divinities differs in 3 instances from
that usually received. Herodotus is so positive that
Herakles is an Egyptian name that I cannot admit
his identity with Khons: nor can Khons come
before Amenra in the list. Har·ka·ra is exactly

transliterated by Her·ak·les; and I believe that Har-ka was the name intended by Herodotus. The patron deity of the Herakleopolite nome, however, was Khnum, who was too important to be omitted in the list of divine kings. I take Khnum, therefore, to have been a demigod in the original list. Har·Shef (?= Har·ka) was patron of Herakleopolis.

It is noticeable that the great gods (including Har) are all of Lower Egypt: Ptah of Memphis, Ra (or Tum) of Heliopolis, Asar of many places but especially of Busiris; Har, his son, of Tanis and other towns; while the demigods are of Upper Egypt: Anhur of Abydos (later on of Sebennytus in the North), Anup of Kynopolis and Lykopolis, Khnum of Elefantine, Herakleopolis, &c.; Haroeris of Apollinopolis, &c. &c., Min (Amsu) of Koptos and Panopolis, Thot of Hermopolis, Sebek of Krokodeilopolis and the Fayum, Amenra of Diospolis (Thebes), Xois, &c. This points to the whole list being an amalgamation of a Memphite and a Theban system, in which the former was preferred. Such amalgamation was not possible till Dyn. xviii.: a likely time for it is the reign of Tahutmes iii.

I do not believe that Shu and Amen occur twice over in the list: Sosos seems to be a variant of Sokhos or Sevekhos, i.e., of Sebek; and Ammon (Zeus being certainly Amenra) is Min, which is a variant writing of the name Amen, as Lepage Renouf has sufficiently demonstrated.

G

HELIOPOLITE SCHEME.

GREEK.	EGYPTIAN.	YEARS.
Hefaistos	Ptah	0—" he shineth night and day "
Helios	Ra	30,000
Kronos, &c.	Seb and the rest of the 12	3984
8 Demigods		217

The near equivalence of the 217 years of the demigods with the 214 of the Memphite scheme shows a common origin. The number 3984 is exactly double of 1992 = 700 Shu + 500 Set + 433 Asar + 359 Set (Memphite): while 30,000 is a further glorification of Ra by making his 30,000 days into years, instead of his 1000 months, as in the Memphite reckoning. I hold that this scheme was subsequent to the Memphite. Ptah is virtually ignored, with a courteous but ineffectual mention.

ANOTHER SCHEME.

	EUSEBIUS.	MEMPHITE.
7 great gods including Harsiesis and a long succession to Bites	13,900	12,288
[8] demigods	1,255	1,200
Kings	1,817	
30 Memphites	1,790	3,650
10 Thinites	350	350
Manes and demigods	5,813	
Sum	24,925	
Sum stated	24,900	
Sum without Manes	19,087	17,488

In this strange scheme preserved by Eusebius Hefaistos is expressly stated to have been the first man (*homo*) who reigned over Egypt. The origin is therefore probably Memphite. The first item, 13,900, is, I suppose, made up of 12,300 for the 7 great gods, as in the Memphite already given, and 1600 for kings of whom we hear in no other place. Neither do we of the Manes, &c., with their 5813 years. The total is 25 years in error; doubtless the round number in such a mythic calculation is the true one. Subtracting this, we have 1230 years for the 8 demigods without Harsiesis, just one-tenth of 12,300 for the 7 gods. The next two items of kings correspond fairly to the 30 Memphite demigods, who have now become mortal, but this tell-tale 30 still left in the text shows whence they were derived. The total without the 1600 + 5813 interpolated years is 17,487 against 17,488 of the earlier scheme. I think this scheme, so arbitrarily artificial, must be very late, certainly later than Manetho. On the other hand, 24,925 + 2075 (the historical period in Eratosthenes) = 27,000, the earliest Egyptian estimate for the precessional period, whose true value is 25,868 years.

SECTION III.

THE SED PERIODS.

AFTER I had finished the writing of this book in 1894 I read Sir Norman Lockyer's "Dawn of Astronomy," and the hypothesis advanced by him that there were two solar cults, one equinoxial, the other solstitial, appeared to me to throw so much light on Egyptian chronology that I deferred publication until I could get sufficient leisure to examine the subject under this new aspect. With his hypotheses on orientation of temples to star-worship I have no concern; they are founded on historical data which are too uncertain to yield any sure basis at present, although his classification of facts may ultimately prove very useful: but his views on solar-worship have resulted in my cancelling the section on Seds as I had then written it and re-arranging the matter so as to serve as a test of my results generally. This may have introduced discrepancies to the extent of one or two years at most in some overlooked passages (for I had to alter early dates by that amount, and have re-written my tables in consequence): if so the dates now to be given are those to which I finally adhere.

The Egyptian year (*annus vagus*) of 365 days is deficient by 5h. 48m. 58s.: in 1508 years or perhaps a year or so less this error amounts to a year, and the seasons occur again in their due place as at first, having passed through 365 changes of a day each in the calendar reckoning. The discrepancy between the calendar and the actual rise of the Nile was noted very early in Egyptian history, certainly as early as 2780 B.C., but it will be more convenient in treating this subject to consider first of all the manner in which they attempted to remedy this defect in later times. My reason for this procedure is that this later correction is the only one generally noticed by chronologers. A very fair first approximation to correctness is obtained by taking the year as 365d. 6h. This is the Julian year: and as the star Sothis (Sirius), owing to its peculiar precessional motion, rises heliacally at intervals of very nearly exact Julian years, and this heliacal rising takes place in Egypt near the time of the Nile rising, it was naturally made the basis of their corrected year. Thus every 4 years gave them 1 day correction: every 28 years 1 week, and every 1460 years 1 year. That is to say, 1460 corrected years were equal to 1461 vague years. This period of 1461 vague years they called a Sothic cycle; and as the times of the heliacal risings of Sirius were determined by actual observation, had they inscribed on their monuments the month-days on which this rising took place we should have no chronological difficulties at all. Unfortunately they scarcely ever did so. We must make the best of such notices as we have.

Censorinus, in his *de Die Natali*, which he began to write in A.D. 238, says that at the date of his writing the *annus vagus* began a.d. 7 Kal. Jul. (June 25), and that 100 years before it began

a.d. 12 Kal. Aug., July 21, on which day *solet
canicula in Ægypto facere exortum.* "Wherefore
this present year is the 100th of the canicular year."
Now, from June 25 to July 21 is 26 days, which
change requires 104 years; therefore there is one
day error. We must read vi. Kal. Jul. or xiii. Kal.
Aug. The latter correction is usually adopted because Censorinus gives his date of writing an earlier
part of his book as A.D. 238. He may, however,
have been four years or more engaged upon it; and
it is impossible in any way to reconcile Mahler's date
1470 or (1471 as corrected by Eisenlohr) for the
28 Epifi Sed under Tahutmes iii. with a Sothic epoch
of 1322 B.C. I therefore, as Oppolzer and others
have done before me, adopt the other correction,
which gives 1318 B.C. as the year for the commencement of this Sothic cycle.

Moreover, we have monumental evidence that on
9 Epifi in the 9th year of Amenhotep i. there was a
Sed festival, and, continuing the calculation from
that year, which was certainly 1547 B.C., we find
1 Thoth 1318 for a true Sed date. The ascription of
the 9 Epifi monument to Amenhotep i. has been
disputed; but not by any one who had not some
hypothesis which it unpleasantly refuted. Other
Seds mentioned but not dated are the following. I
insert the dates from calculation :

B.C.	Sed Day.	Year of King.	Sed.
1547	9 Epifi	9 Amenhotep i.	44
[1519	16 Epifi	Tahutmes i.	45
1435	7 Mesore	Amenhotep ii.	48
1407	14 Mesore	Amenhotep iii.	49
1351	28 Mesore	Tutankhamen	51
1234	22 Thoth	41 Ramessu ii.	3
1206	29 Thoth	2 Merenptah	4
926	9 Khoiak]	2 Usarkhon i.	14

All of these will be found to fall within the reigns required; which, considering the extreme shortness of some of them, is a strong testimony to the truth of my chronology for this period.

Of course the 52nd Sed falls on Epact 5, 1323, and the new cycle begins on 1 Thoth, 5 years after, to make up the odd day over 52 weeks in the year. This would not be worth mention had not some chronologers of the highest merit as "diggers" and antiquarians fallen into the error of making Thoth 7, 14, &c., fall on Sed days. The year 1319 is the intercalary vague year, which marks the equality of 1461 vague years and 1460 fixed years: 1318 begins the new cycle.

So far I have had little to add to the theory of Seds and cycles as set forth by others. I have to dissent from my predecessors *in toto* for the rest of this chapter. Norman Lockyer quotes from the monuments a statement that there was a Sed held in the reign of Pepy ii. on 27 Epifi; he treats this date as a discrepancy of little import, and other historians and chronologers seem to have neglected it altogether.

To me it has the highest significance, for it shows
that in the Memphite period the Sed epoch was not
1 Thoth at all, for that leads to 30 Epifi, not 27.
There must have been at this time an entirely
different system in use. Lockyer himself has shown
the probability that the names of the hieroglyphs for
the seasons were changed; that which now corresponds to Thoth and the 3 sequent months having
originally belonged to Tybi; for Thoth, the month of
Nile rise, has the sign that would naturally indicate
seed time. Accordingly, if we reckon backward
from 27 Epifi for 22 Seds, we reach 1 Tybi for a feast
day, and this is no doubt the true reckoning. For
if we reckon forward the first month-day or epoch
will fall on 1 Athyr (or 1 Payni), which does not
head a season group at all. It is most unlikely that
any epoch should have been used outside 1 Thoth,
1 Tybi, 1 Pakhons, unless it be 1 Famenoth, as
representing the winter solstice. The other 8 months
are excluded. And we have a perfect right to reckon
backward: the priests may have registered the day
in the vague year, on which the epoch day (e.g.,
1 Thoth) was celebrated: or they may have registered the day in the Sothic year, on which the epoch
day of the vague year occurred : and these reckonings
proceed respectively forward or backward. Indeed
Lockyer makes them always go backward: while
Egyptologers generally reckon always forward. In
my scheme they reckon forward under the Theban
kings on the Thoth system, but backward under
the Memphite on the Tybi method. There are also
3 monumental records of Sed festivals giving regnal

years—viz., 2 xi. 9 Nebtauira i., 22 vi. 5 Pepy i., and
3 xii. 2 Usertsen i.—which fell in my calculation on
2181, 2151, 2031 B.C. respectively. Therefore the
Sed epoch fell on 2781, 2751, or 2721, according as
we take the Sed on 27 Epifi to have been the 1st,
2nd, or 3rd Sed under Pepy ii. I think the second
date the most likely. The complete scheme for Tybi
Seds is as follows : but a variation of 1 Sed either
way is possible :

B.C.	SED DAY.	YEAR OF KING.	SED.
2241	[2 Thoth	Dadkara Assa	17
2181	18 Mesore	22 Nebtauira	19
2151	11 Mesore]	18 Pepy i.	20
2121	4 Mesore	Pepy ii.	21
2091	[27 Epifi	,,	22
2061	20 Epifi	,,	23
2031	13 Epifi]	3 Usertesen i.	24

The Seds in this system proceed by intervals of
30 years, not 28, and we know that for this period
the little or sacred year of 360 days was in use.
The system is palpably different from the Sothic in
every respect. If founded on the year of 360 days,
as it surely must have been (for what else was there
to found on ?), the cycle would be 51 weeks of
30 years each + 12 or 13 years for the 3 odd days :
$(51 \times 7 + 3 = 360)$; and the cycle would consist of
$51 \times 30 + 13$ or 1543 years. Now on the ceiling in
the Ramesseum at Thebes there is a representation
of the heavens, which was made under Ramessu ii.,
and which was by most modern chronologers
mistaken for a map of the stars at the end of a

Sothic cycle, at 1 Thoth. Eisenlohr has shown that this is not the case; the "anap" in the map does not occur in the Thoth month, as it should do on that hypothesis, but in Tybi. This exactly agrees with my theory of the Tybi Seds, for the end of a cycle of 1543 years from 2751 B.C. would come in 1208 or the 67th year of Ramessu ii. If 2781 were the original epoch, the results would be quite as satisfactory; for the known fact that Ramessu ii. celebrated Seds in his 30th, 33rd, 37th, and 41st years, leaves little doubt that some one of them would be the beginning of a new Sed cycle beginning on 1 Tybi. It is possible that these frequent Seds of this king were the result of an attempt to combine the various systems in use before his time, rather than merely personal glorification, as they are usually esteemed.

The singularly exact coincidence of all the known Sed dates of this second series with my system deduced on totally different grounds, and the absolute failure of any other system yet proposed to satisfy this test, gives me great confidence in the truth of my results.

Yet once more, there is a third system of Seds in which a Sed is recorded as falling on neither the 27th nor the 30th, but on the 28th of Epifi. This was in 1471, the 33rd year of Tahutmes iii. Only one other Sed is known as belonging to this system, although it is possible that the undated Seds under Amenhotep ii., iii., which I have placed in the Sothic series, may be here included. The interval between the 2 Seds is 28; the cycle is therefore of 1460 years. If we reckon back 21 Seds from 28 Epifi it brings us to 1 Famenoth, and this is doubtless the epoch of this system. The epoch date will then be $21 \times 28 + 1471 = 2059$ B.C.

1499	[21 Epifi	16 Hatshepsut	20 from epoch
1471	28 Epifi	33 Tahutmes iii.	21

This system starts as near as observations of Sirius would permit from the foundation of Dyn xii., 2053 B.C.

Even this is not all. There is, as we shall presently see, evidence that Sothic cycles were reckoned in later times from 2031 or 2024 B.C. Now cycles of 1460 years depend on actual observation of heliacal risings of Sirius; and this rising in 2059 took place on 1 Famenoth, in 2031 on 8 Famenoth. This system, then, points to a winter solstitial cult, and I may note by the way that, though not introduced here as not belonging to my present subject, I have deduced some results from this, which strongly confirm Lockyer's hypotheses on winter solstice orientation. As these later cycles are only found in priestly calculations of the Manethonic type, and were never publicly observed, exact agreement with true dates is not to be expected, and it would be sheer waste of time to examine the exaggerated numbers of this school from this point of view.

Closely connected with the Sed problem is the question of the inscription under Ramessu ii. in the 400th year of Set·aa·pehti Nubti·set. Ramessu ii.

reigned 1274–1207 : Set·aa therefore falls between
1674 and 1607.   Now the supreme kings for this
time were St·aa·n 1679–1629, Assis 1629–1580.
Surely St·aa·n must be Set·aa·nub.   But it is to
A·seth (Assis)=Aa·seh that the change from the
year of 360 days to that of 365 is attributed in
Synkellos.   This of course is absurd if taken *lite-
ratim :* the Epacts had been in use from the
beginning of Dyn. xii., but it is quite possible
that the change from the Sed system, which
reckoned years of 360 days (from 1 Tybi), to the
Sothic system, which reckoned 365 (from 1 Thoth)
took place at this time.   The only way to account
for the introduction of Staan and Assis indiscrimi-
nately as authors of this change is to place its
exact date at the junction of their reigns.   Thus
Staan promulgates the new system in his last year
(1631) ; Assis (in conjunction with Kertos, his
assessor) carries it out from 1629 onwards and
celebrates the first Sed of this Sothic scheme in
1603.   The epoch of Staan is 1631, that of
Ramses ii. 1231, his 43rd year.   All the conditions of the problem are fulfilled ; and I ask the
reader to compare any other modern chronological
system and see how it fails in definiteness at this
point.   This 400-year method of epoch dates at
least from 2031, the Sed year of Usertsen i., which
was the beginning of the use of Epacts at all.

[Again, in the 30th year of Usertsen i. Amenemhat, son of Nehera, was sent to get alabaster
at Hat Nub on a Sed day.   I have above assumed
that the obelisk erected in the beginning of the Sed

festival at Heliopolis was of the same date as the temple—3rd year of Usertsen i.; as there cannot be less than 28 years between 2 Seds of the same system, the obelisk must have been set up in the 2nd year. The year, however, 2031, need not be changed: it fell partly in the 2nd, partly in the 3rd year of the reign. The importance of this notice is that 2031 belonged to the 30 year system from 1 Tybi, and also to the 28 year system from 1 Famenoth: according with my conjecture in the body of the text. Addition made March 1899.]

I now recapitulate these results in chronological order.

2781 or 2751 B.C.—Sed festivals were established on 1 Tybi. The only year in use was the little one of 360 days. The cycle consisted of 1543 years. There may have been observations of some star whose precession was in the opposite direction to that of Sirius taken in connexion with these festivals; but this astronomical question would require an investigation too long to be included in the present essay. The first Sed falls in the reign of Kakaa, to whom the deification of the sacred bulls is attributed by Manetho.

2031 B.C.—The Epacts were introduced into civil reckoning by Arminon (Ra Ameny Antef), and this year was long afterwards reckoned as the epoch of Arminon: Sed festival henceforth reckoned from 1 Famenoth 2059.

1631 B.C.—The $365\frac{1}{4}$ days for the year were introduced by Staan (Set Aa Nubti) in Sed reckonings from 1 Thoth 2779, and the Sothic cycle was adopted of 1461 years. This year was the epoch of Staan.

c. 1501 B.C. — Hatshepsut revived the cycle reckoned from 1 Famenoth, 2059 ; but this was only used during her reign and that of Thotmes iii.

Shortly after this the first ancestral genealogy was formed, as we have it in the temple of Karnak.

1318 B.C.—A new Sothic cycle begins in the reign of Ramessu i., Men·peh·ra. This is another epoch, that of Menofres, who is now admitted to have been this king.

1238 or 1208 B.C.—A new Tybi cycle begins in 37th or 67th year of Ramessu ii., and was celebrated by a Sed festival commemorated on a ceiling in the Ramesseum.

1231 B.C.—The 400th year from the Staan epoch was recorded in the 44th year of Ramessu ii.

571 B.C.—The Saite priests calculate Sothic cycles from Mena, 3491, to Usertsen i., 2031, and to Aahmes (xxvi. 8) 571; but the festivals of these cycles are not recorded as ever receiving public recognition.

238 B.C.—The celebrated decree of Canopus, changing the cyclic epoch from 1 Thoth to 1 Pakhons, lies beyond the scope of this essay : but it requires notice on account of the inscription at Philæ, in which 1 Thoth is stated as falling on 28 Epifi. The date at which this inscription was made must have been between 127 and 117 (Brugsch). Now if Brugsch is right in his date, this implies some reckoning unknown elsewhere : for it agrees neither with the decree nor with any hieratic calendar. No explanation that is satis-

factory has come under my notice. But as this 28 Epifi is probably not of a Sed festival year, we need not discuss the matter further in this place.

I append a table of Sed days, to aid the reader in checking my calculations :

1	8	15	22	29	1 Thoth		1 Famenoth
	6	13	20	27		27 Epifi	[21 Seds of
	4	11	18	25	[47 Seds of		28 years taken
2	9	16	23	30	28 years	[22 Seds of	downwards]
	7	14	21	28	taken	30 years	28 Epifi
	5	12	19	26	downwards]	upwards]	
	3	10	17	24			
1	8	15	22	29		1 Tybi	
	6	13	20	27			
	4	11	18	25			
2	9	16	23	30	30 Epifi		
	7	14	21	28			
	5						

SECTION IV.

THE ANCIENT SCHEMES OF CHRONOLOGY.

1. ERATOSTHENES.

THE ancient schemes assign to Mena dates varying from 2600 B.C. to 3681. I shall discuss them in the order of these Mena dates, and not in that of their historic development; their interconnexion being more apparent in this method. Eratosthenes, who lived under the Ptolemies 276–196 B.C., gives from Apollonius a list of 38 kings (Dyn. i.–x.) which I reproduce in full, and add the names of those which can be certainly identified from the other lists or monuments :

KINGS.	TITLES, &c.	YEARS.	DYN.	KINGS.
1. Menes	Thebinites, Thebaios, Aionios	62	i. 1	Mena
2. Athothis	his son. Hermogenes	59	2	Teta
3. Athothes	his son	32	3	Ateth
4. Diabies	his son. Filetairos (true to friends)	19	6	Miebis
5. Pemfos	son of Athothis. Herakleides	18	7	Semempses
	Sum	190		
6. Toegar	Amakos (unconquered), Momkeiri, Memfites, Telandros (?) Perissomakos (?)	79	ii. 1	Bezau
7. Stoikhos	Ares anaisthetos	6	2	Kaiekhos
8. Gosormies	Etesipantos	30		
9. Mares	Heliodoros	26		
10. Anoyfis	Epikomos (hairy)	20		
	Sum	161		
11. Sirios	Uios Kores, or Abaskantos (unenvied)	18	iii. 1	Nebka (?)
12. Knoubis	Gneuros; Khruses (Khruson) uios	22	2	Zesersa
13. Rauosis	Arkhikrator	13	3	Zeserteta
	Sum	53		
14. Biyris		10	iv. 1	Soris
15. Saofis i.	Komastes (reveller) or Khrematestes (money getter)	29	2	Soyfis
	Sum to here	443		
16. Saofis ii.		27	3	Soyfis
17. Moskhares	Heliodotos	31	4	Menkheres
	Sum	97		

KINGS.	TITLES, &C.	YEARS.	DYN.	KINGS.
18. Mousthis		33	v.	
19. Pammes	Arkhondes	35	,,	
	Sum	68		
20. Apappos	Megistos (all but 1 hour)	100	vi. 5	Fiops
21. Ekheskosokaras		1	6	Menthesoufis
22. Nitokris	Athene nikeferos Anti tou androsandros	6	8	Netaqerti
	Sum	107		
23. Myrtaios	Ammonodotos	22	vii.	
24. Thyosimares	Krataios = Helios	12	viii.	Dadkashemara
25. Thinillos	Auxesas to patrion Kratos	8		
26. Semfroukrates	Herakles Harpokrates	18		Sneferkara
27. Khuther	Tauros tyrannos	7		Raenka
28. Meures	Filoskoros	12		
29. Khoimaiftha	Kosmos filefaistos	11		
30. Soikyniosokhos	Tyrannos	60		
31. Peteathyres		16	(22)	
	Sum	166	(192)	
32. Stammenemes ii.	[Akhthoes = Khety]	23	ix. 1	Abmeryra
	[the rest of ix. omitted]			
33. Sistosikhermes	Herakles Krataios	55	x. 1	
34. Maris		43		
35. Sifoas	Hermes ; uios Hefaistou	5		
36. —		} 14	(19)	
37. Frouron	= Neilos			
38. Amouthantaios		63		
	Sum	180	(185)	

39-91 : 53 other " Theban " kings ; names and dates not given.

For this list there are 2 various readings ; usually passed over in silence, but to me they seem full of significance.

The statement in Synkellos is that he reckoned 38 kings and 1076 years from A.M. 2900 to 3045 ;

H

a most contradictory assertion.   We must of course
read 3945, but this leaves the 1045 years from
A.M. 2900 to 3945 irreconcilable with 1076.

Again, in the list itself we find the following :

31. Peteathyres	16 years	A.M. 3726
32. Stammenemes ii	23 „	A.M. 3768 .

Where the years actually counted are not 16 but 42.
Again, p. 233 :

35. Sifoas	5 years	A.M. 3889
[36.]		
37. Frouron	5 „	A.M. 3889
38. Amouthantaios	63 „	A.M. 3913
		A.M. 3976

Instead of the second " 5 years A.M. 3889," which
is an erroneous repetition from the preceding line, we
are bound to insert " 19 years," thus,

35. Sifoas	5 years	A.M. 3889
36. —	19 „	A.M. 3884
37. Frouron		
38.		A.M. 3913

to rectify the received text, which reckons 1076
years in all : but the other reckoning of 1045 years
would require here only 14 years, not 19, to be
inserted.   It is clear that the shorter reckoning is
the original version of Eratosthenes, and that the
31 additional years were inserted by some corrector.
By doing this he obtained an agreement for Dyn. x.
with Manetho's 185 years, a round number of 400
for Dyn. vii.–x., and a total of 215 for vii.–ix.   This
looks like the work of some post-Christian hand who
made Abraham contemporary with Myrtaios, Jacob's
Eisode with xi., and dated the Exodus in the 5th
year of Khebron's reign.   This would not be far from
Africanus' scheme.

Eratosthenes then reckoned 1045 years from 2600 B.C. (A.M. 2900 of Synkellos to 1555, the beginning of Dyn. xviii. if Aahmes be not reckoned), and he had after this a list of 53 kings, which has not come down to us. These must have been the kings from Khebron to Kambyses (xviii.–xxvi.), when for the first time a foreign power conquered the whole of Egypt in 525 B.C. Eratosthenes' scheme therefore embraced in all 2075 years: he does not count Dyn. xx., nor Amenofath xviii. 16. Referring to the 3rd scheme for the divine dynasties, which cannot have belonged to any extant chronology but that of Eratosthenes, all the others being already otherwise provided for, we find the total divine reigns occupied 24,900 years. But $24,900 = 12 \times 2075$: the gods reign as many years as the men kings do months. Is not this, again, a disguising of history like that we have already met with in the Memphite scheme? Can such an exact agreement be merely accidental?

2. THE CHRONICLE.

Ra	. . .	. 30,000 years
Gods	. . .	. 3,984 „
Demigods	. .	. 217 „
Kings	. .	. 2,324 „
	Total .	. 36,525 „

This chronography had 30 dynasties and 113 generations (*geneai*), and consisted of Aurites, Mestræans, and Egyptians. As it certainly ended 341 B.C. at the accession of Okhos the Persian, its epoch for Menes is 2665. The king list is as follows:

Dyn.		Years.
i.–iv.	15 geneai of the Cynic cycle	443
v.	8 Tanites	190
vi.	4 Memphites	103
vii.–x.	14 ,,	348
xviii.	{ [9] Diospolites	194
	{ 5 ,,	[50]
xix.	8 ,,	228
xxi.	[7 Tanites	128]
xxii.	{ 6 ,,	121
	{ 3 ,,	48
xxiii.	2 Diospolites	19
xxiv.	3 Saites	44
xxv.	3 Ethiopians	44
xxvi.	7 Memphites	177
xxvii.	5 Persians	124
xxviii.	1 Saite	[6]
xxix.	[7] Mendesians	39
xxx.	1 Tanite	18
Total	108 (stated 113)	2324
Add	8 Demigods	217
	(121)	2541

The grand total is here made up of 25 Sothic periods of 1461 years: but the numbers seem also to be based on a reckoning by units of 21 years. The years of the gods, 3984, and demigods, 217, form a total of 4201 or 200×21, the end year being reckoned as current: the demigods' 217, with the years of the two first dynasties, which I have shown under "Dynasties" to be 350, make 567 or 27×21; the remaining years to the end of Dynasty xxx. are $1974 = 94 \times 21$. The whole king period (including the demigods) is therefore 121 average reigns of 21 years each, and the subtraction of the 8 demigods gives the 113 reigns which the Chronicle assigns to the men dynasties. This does not quite agree with the sum of the kings in his table, but this must be examined separately.

Moreover, there is another reckoning—that by Sed periods of 30 years—which also underlies the Chronicler's numbers. The time of Helios is 1000 such periods : that of the gods and demigods 140 such ; that from the first demigod to the end of what the Chronicler calls the Cynic cycle is 660 years, or 22 Seds : from this point to the commencement of the Sothic cycle, wrongly taken as 1322 B.C., is 30 Seds ; and from thence to the conquest of Egypt by Alexander is 33 Seds.

By adding the demigods we can clearly trace the genesis of the number 217, and the meaning of *genea* (generation) which Eusebius and the moderns agree in interpreting as "dynasty." For $121 \times 21 = 2541$; 121 *geneai* of 21 years each make up the sum 2541. Now, 21 years is a very good number for an average reign, and has the advantage of 2 mystic numbers, 3 and 7, for its factors. Thus subtracting the 8 demigod reigns with 217 years, we get the 113 reigns and 2324 years stated in Synkellos. But we do not get 30 dynasties, and as the Chronicle cannot have more than 20, even reckoning xxii. as two, for vii.–x. can reckon for one only, I have no hesitation in ascribing this number to a later hand, probably Eusebius, who introduced the absurd numbering of the dynasties.

This scheme was made evidently after the accession of Okhos the Persian, and very likely during his reign. Its artificial character down to xviii. is evident : the manipulation of the divine numbers ·

as previously shown is very ingenious. From xviii. onward it accords closely with historic fact.

The hypothesis that this "ancient chronography extant among the Egyptians" was post-Christian, as is sometimes asserted by writers who are prejudiced by anti-Biblical theories, has no shadow of evidence to support it. It is a mere pronouncement *ex cathedra*.

In filling up the lost numbers of kings those for xviii., xxi. are certain: and for xxix. I include Mouthis (omitted by Africanus). There is still a deficiency of 5 to make up the stated 113, which is undoubtedly right. I would suggest reading vii.-x. 16 Memphites (the number in Eratosthenes: all other authorities have still higher numerals), and xxvii. 8 Persians, as all the Manethonic lists have it.

3. THE TURIN PAPYRUS.

The only entry of divine reigns that has survived is that of the Shemsu Hor for 13,420 years + some tens or units that are lost. The similarity of this number to the 13,900 in the Eratosthenes scheme for 7 great gods and kings to Bites looks as if the Turin numbers were for "[7 gods and] Shemsu Hor," these followers of Harsiesis being equivalent to the kings from Hor to Bites. But there is also a list of numbers in the papyrus : 73, 74, 83, 95,—,95, 70, 74?, 70 = 325 + 309 = 634, which can hardly be anything else than years of divine reigns. They have, it is true, been assigned to Dyn. i., ii., with a vain hope of bolstering up the

conjectural reading of 1755 for the years from Mena
to the end of Dyn. vi., but are quite insufficient for
the purpose.   This much is certain : these items are
not modified or derived in any way from the Memphite
scheme. But the sum of them corresponds remarkably
with that scheme, which has

7 great gods (including Horus) . .	12,300 years.
8 demigods (seasons column) . .	760 (756)
4 others.	370
Sum . .	13,430 (13,426)

which exactly agrees with the Turin number.   The
Turin items would then belong to 8 out of the 12
demigods who followed Harsiesis, but not calculated
in the Memphite method. I shall examine this point
more fully further on.

The men kings may be thus tabulated :

i.–vi. 755	xi. 243	xii. 213	xiv. [184]
vii.–x. 355	xiii. [?]	xvii. 151	xv. [?]

The numbers in the first column are expressly
stated, but unfortunately the *terminus ad quem*
is not precisely known : we are not informed exactly
where Dyn. x. ends, and there is not perfect agreement on this point in the other authorities : Manetho
ends it in 1580, the accession of Aahmes : Eratosthenes in 1555, the accession of Khebron ; the
Chronicler in 1580 ; and this, I think, is also the
epoch used in the Turin papyrus. If so, the years
from the death of Nitokris to the accession of
Aahmes would be 355 + 14 = 369, agreeing with

Eratosthenes' 369 in number, but not in epoch. All these short schemes agree in omitting the time during which the Hyksos were supreme.

But it will be said, if this system of contemporaneous dynasties be true, there ought in the Turin scheme to be similar omissions of 89 years in the other columns, and therefore in Dyn. xiii. and xv., since xi. and xiv. were almost certainly given in full. Well, I cannot say anything as to xv., as only 2 reigns can be identified in the list; but as to xiii. there is such an omission. Eight kings at least, including the important Sebekemsafs (Nos. 39–47) are proved by the Karnak list to have reigned, of whom there is no trace in the Turin, and these kings are in my calculation contemporary with xv. This batch of kings in Dyn. xiii. and the group v. 1–5 are the only kings in the whole period i.–xvii. of whom no trace, direct or inferential, is to be found in any of the 164 fragments of this mutilated document. Moreover, the full list of the short reckoning and the Manethonic reckoning from B.C. 2024–1580, which have enabled me to evolve the system now presented, indicate only the following deficiencies in the Turin list: (1) a possible lowering of the numbers in i. or ii. by 52 years, if the Manethonic numbers for those lost in the Turin list be correctly substituted. (2) An omission of 125 years for v. 1–5. (3) An omission of 89 years in ix. and its cotemporaries xiii., xv. In all other respects this document is faultless. In no one instance has a discrepancy between it and any authentic monument ever been discovered. Is it likely, then, that such an omission as 125 years concerning kings whose monuments exist even now could have been made by its compiler ?   I think not, and in my final results I will give my hypothetic explanation.

The Abydos tablet, which was set up under Ramessu ii., differs from the Turin scheme only in having 4 additional kings—Teta, Sememptah, Bezau, and Neterkara.   As their united reigns make 104 years$=47+18+38+1$, this would seem to be founded on a cycle of $52 \times 30+4=1564$, instead of $52 \times 28+4=1460$.   But this " 104 years " was made up of supposititious kings, unknown outside this table and that of Sakkara, which is merely an incomplete and not accurate copy of it.

4. SAITE (FROM HERODOTUS).

The remaining schemes belong to the long chronology, and are all modifications of a single scheme.   As the only extant complete lists are those of Manetho, handed down in an altered form by Africanus and Eusebius, it may seem Quixotic to attempt to reproduce the earlier versions entire.   Nevertheless, the indications given us in stray hints in Herodotus and Synkellos, combined with the peculiar numerical relations of the items, will, I believe, make it possible. For convenience of reference I give here a table of my ultimate results for all these Manethonic schemes :

DYN.	SAITE.	MANETHO.	REDACTOR.	AFRICANUS.	EUSEBIUS.	
			SUMS.	ITEMS.	SUMS.	ITEMS.
i.	253	253	253	263	252	228
ii.	302	302	302	302	297	
iii.	214	214	214	214	197	
iv.	277	277	27[7]	284)	[5]48	
v.	218	218	248	218)		
vi.	197	197	203	203	203	
Sum	1461	1461	1497	1484	1497	
xi.	—	—	—	43		
xii.1	14	—	16	16		(16
xii.	182	182	184	160	200	(182
xv.	260	260	260	284	250	(= xvii.)
Sum	456	444	460	503	450	
xvii.	—	—	—	151	103	(= xv.)
xviii.	263	263	263	262	348	317
xix.	209	209	209	205	194	162
xx.	—	—	—	135	172	
xx A.	—	—	[143]	[143]	—	—
xxi.	130	130	130	114	130	
xxii.	118	118	120	116	—	
	[48	48	48	48]	4[9]	49
xxiii.	89	89	89	89	44	
xxiv.	6	6	6	6	44	
xxv.	40	40	40	40	44	
xxvi.	100	106	106	106	125	129
Sum	1003	1009	1154	1272	1253	
Aahmes		44,6	44,6	44,6	42,0	
xxvii.		120,4	124,4	124,4	120,4	
xxviii.		6,0	6,0	6,0	6,0	
xxix.		20,4	20,4	20,4	21,4	
xxx.		38,0	38,0	38,0	38,0	
Sum		229,2	233,2	233,2	227,8	

I begin with Herodotus' scheme, derived from the Saite priests :

NAMES.	NUMBER.	YEARS.	HERODOTUS
Hefaistos (Ptah)	—	9,000	—
Helios (Ra) and 4	5	3,000	—
Herakles (Har) and 11	12	1,870	2.000 = 17,000 − 15,000
Dionysos and 29	30	3,650	3,560 = 15,000 − 11,340
Menes to Sethos	331	2,820	11,340
xxvi. 1-7	—	100	100
Sum	378	20,440	

The numbers given by Herodotus are usually thrown aside as valueless ; I regard them as important, because I believe that under them is concealed a proof that Manetho derived his dynastic items from a scheme as early at least as Amosis, xxvi. 8, B.C. 571. Herodotus says that the priests reckoned 11,340 years for 131 generations from Menes to Sethos ; and, again, 15,000 years from Dionysos, whom he places at the head of his third class of deities (*i.e.*, of the 30 demigods), to the epoch of Amosis : and, again, from Herakles, whom he puts at the head of the 12 demigods to the same epoch, 17,000 years. This gives us the numbers as I have tabulated them. The 2000 years from Herakles to Dionysos may well be a round statement for the 1870 for Horus and the other 11 demigods ; but cannot be identified with any other items of the Memphite scheme. He must have confused Horus, the young sun (Harsiesis) with the infant Herakles (Harkara) ; for Herakles, the 4th demigod, cannot be made the head of any group of 12 deities. Then his number 3560 years for the third class is almost certainly to be identified with the 3650 of the Memphite scheme, seeing that it is not stated explicitly, but deduced from a statement which already gives one round number as an approximation. But the 11,340 years cannot be right; there is no trace of such an exaggerated period of men kings to be found in Egyptian chronology elsewhere. I believe that he mistook the priests' statement, that from the time of their first king to the end of Sethos made up* 11,340 years— *i.e.*, 378 Seds or generations of 30 years for 378 kings: and that they meant their first god-king Ra, while he understood their first man king, Menes. If this be so, and surely the mistake is likely enough, the priests reckoned 11,440 years from Ra to Amosis as I have given in the "years" column: this requires exactly two Sothic periods from Menes to Amosis, and agrees within 8 years with the list of Africanus, as we have it in the items. Even these 8 years can be accounted for. Herodotus has 25 years for Vafres xxvi. 7, Africanus 19: and Manetho has an error of two years in his epoch for Kambyses.

As every number in the years column is taken from the original scheme of the priests (*cf.* Lepsius, *Königsbuch*, I. Taf. iii.), I feel no doubt that these Memphites arranged so as to get 14 Sothic periods $= 14 \times 1460 = 20,440$, from Hefaistos, 2 from Menes $= 2 \times 1460 = 2920$, and $4\frac{1}{2}$ from Dionysos $= 9 \times 730 =$

---

* Or possibly 405 Seds of 28 years.

6570.   Consequently all the corruptions in the early dynasties i.–vi. were due to them, and not even for the unauthorised insertions in his third volume is Manetho responsible : as we shall see.

I take the statement in Herodotus ii. 142, that the sun had twice risen where he now sets, and twice set where he now rises, to mean that two complete Sothic cycles had been gone through since the time of Menes; and that the priests simply told Herodotus that the heliacal rising of Sirius had twice run through its course of change.   The number of kings (341) is, I believe, a deduction by Herodotus from his way of estimating generations as three in a century, which would require 11,367 years instead of 11,340 : the true number is doubtless 331, as given before by him in chap. 100.   For his total of years to the end of Dyn. xxv. is 11,340=378 generations of 30 years each, and the number of his kings from Ra is 5 great gods, 12 demigods, 30 of the third class; which, with 331 men kings, makes up 378 kings to correspond with these 378 generations. Moreover, the number of kings in Manetho (including his contemporary dynasties) agrees with this 331, if certain corrections, otherwise necessary, be made in them.

Under the heading of Manethonic Kings I shall show that Manetho's reckoning was for vol. i. 92 kings; for vol. ii. 196; and for vol. iii. to Amosis there are 43 : total 331, exactly Herodotus' number.

The 18 Ethiopians mentioned by Herodotus I take to include all foreign usurpers, viz., 6 Hyksos, xv.: 9 Semites (?) xxii.: and 3 Ethiopians, xxv.

The priests may have said to him : "Eighteen
strangers, such as Ethiopians," or words to that
effect.

I may also note, while mentioning Herodotus,
that his historical inaccuracy of which so much has
been lately alleged to his discredit, on examination
is reduced to a single item—a misplacement of the
pyramid-building kings : if these (Kheops, Khefren,
Mykerinos, and Asykhis) are transferred from their
position after Rampsinitos to their proper place
after Menes, the whole of Herodotus' narrative falls
into correct historical succession, and nothing is
proved against him more than an accidental or at
most a mistaken misplacement of a batch of notes on a
definite group of kings ; probably obtained separately
and with imperfect indications of their true historical
relations.

The B.C. dates for the chief epochs under this
scheme will be Menes, 3491 ; Amenemhat i., 2031
(the important Sed festival of 3 or 2 Usertsen i.) ;
Aahmes, 1574 (should be 1580, but the erroneous
reckoning for Vafres already noted has slightly
disorganised this scheme) ; and Amosis, 571. From
the detailed examination of the dynasties it is clear
that the exaggerations in Dyn. i.–vi. were obtained
by introducing kings utterly unknown to any monument, by arbitrarily increasing the regnal years
(sometimes absolutely in contradiction of the monuments), and by reckoning co-regents as if they were
successions. The short chronologies had only to
omit in order to obtain their mystic cycles ; the
long ones had to falsify the old dates and to forge

new ones; but both alike persisted from Ramessu i.
onward in getting by hook or crook some combina-
tion of cycles to start from the first king of Egypt
and end at the epoch of the regnant monarch.

5. MANETHO.

This system is so like the preceding that I need
only note the slight variations.   We have the direct
authority of Synkellos (ignored by modern chronologers) that Manetho's first Sothic cycle (1461 years)
ended in 2024 B.C. (the epoch of Usertsen i.).   He
therefore omitted Amenemhat i. altogether.   But
he had the true reckoning for Vafres : which partially
compensated for this alteration.   His dates are
Menes, 3485 ; Amenemhat i., 2024 (these two are
fixed by Synkellos' statement) ; Aahmes, 1582 ;
Amosis, 573 (each two years in excess) ; Okhos the
Persian, 344.   Every variation in the numbers here
given from those in Africanus will be treated as it
occurs.

This scheme was formed under Ptolemy i. or ii. :
but the grand total, 11,985 years (for the great gods)
+ 214 for the demigods + 3141 for the men kings =
15,340 = 21 × 730.   These 21 semi-Sothics point to
the end of Manetho's scheme as coincident with the
end of the native monarchy.   It was left to his
Redactor to include the Ptolemies in a sacred calculation.

6. THE REDACTOR (AFRICANUS' SUMS).

This is the scheme of the sums stated for each dynasty in Africanus. I have already proved that in this system (and also at first in Africanus) there was a dynasty of 143 years interpolated. Other unauthorised additions are 30 years in v., 6 years in vi. (by making the "reign" of Pepy ii. 100 years instead of his "life"), and 4 years in xxvi., which are discordant with known historical facts. The two years each added to xii. and xxii. are most likely genuine corrections of slight errors : and so is the restoration of the later part of Amenemhat's reign : but I doubt if his amount of 16 years is right ; 14 would exactly agree with the years for the last 4 kings in Dyn. vi. in the Turin list, and with my restoration of the Herodotean scheme, and with the Karnak order for xi. ; as, however, I have used this 16 years throughout this treatise I am fearful of introducing new errors by attempting to correct the numerous places in which it occurs : and in so small a matter (2 years) I trust this notification may be deemed sufficient.

By these additions (200 years in all) the Redactor succeeded in throwing back the dates thus : Menes. 3683 ; Amenemhat i., 2189 ; Aahmes, 1729 ; Amosis, 575 ; Okhos the Persian being taken nearly rightly as 342. All this wanton alteration regardless of historic truth was evidently made to get Sothic cycles ending at 246, which is the epoch of Ptolemy iii., in whose reign this precious absurdity was evolved.

The main epochs are these :

B.C.		YEARS.	
3897	Horus and demigods	214 $\rbrace$	
3683	Menes	516	
3167	Sesokhris = Sesostris	1460	1st Phœnix
1707	Aahmes (end of Hyksos)	1365	2nd ,,
	Sum to Okhos	3555	
342	Okhos the Persian, &c.	95	
247	Sum to Ptolemy iii.	3650	3rd ,,

And this agrees with Tacitus' statement that in one reckoning the Phœnix appeared under Sesostris, Amasis, and Ptolemy iii.

The well known passage of Tacitus (Annals, vi. 28) on the Phœnix runs thus : There are various traditions as to the number of years ; by far the most generally received is that there were intervals of 500 ; some assert that they were of 1461 [a Sothic cycle] and that the earliest birds appeared in the reigns of (1) Sesostris, (2) Amasis, (3) Ptolemy, the third king of the Macedonian dynasty.   Now as Manetho wrote under Ptolemy i. or ii. he could not be the author of this latter statement: it must have arisen under Ptolemy iii., and was, I think, framed by the Redactor. No chronological scheme whatever will allow of Sothic cycles between Sesostris (xii. 3), Amasis (xxvi. 8) and Ptolemy iii. ; but if we reckon the cycles backward in the list of the Redactor they fall in the reigns of Amosis (xviii. 1), who drove out the Hyksos ; and Sesokhris (ii. 8), who is the Sesostris of Herodotus, a mythical double of the historical Sesostris, to whom

I

the conquests of the latter have been attributed with additions, and who is in the list itself sufficiently identified with him by his height of 5 cubits or 4 cubits 3 palms 2 inches. The same regnal years (48) are also attributed to both kings. It is, therefore, evident that the scheme of the Redactor fulfils the required conditions. And now we can easily show how this scheme was framed. Starting from Horus, 3896 B.C., the Phœnix dates are 3166 B.C. (a half Sothic from Horus) for Sesokhris; 1706 B.C. for Amosis; 246 B.C. for Ptolemy iii.; and the correctness of the starting point is proved by the 3555 years total given for this scheme : for $3896 - 3555 = 341$ B.C., the exact epoch of the end of Dynasty xxx. There can be surely no doubt now of the intention of the Ptolemaic chronologer who arranged this scheme.

7. JOSEPHUS.

The numbers in Josephus professedly taken from Manetho are as given in the Table on the next page.

The B.C. dates are calculated from Josephus' known date for the Exodus. The insertion of 60 years is necessary to obtain the given total 393 years from Tethmosis to the brothers. Josephus does not bring the Eisode in the reign of Apofis, and even makes Abraham's visit fall within the Hyksos' time in 2111 B.C.; his 251 years for the later Hyksos may have been the origin of Eusebius' Dyn. xv. 250 years. The years for Al·i·sfr·ag·mou·thosis (Ra·uaz·khpr·ka·mes and certainly not Aahmes·pahar·nub·thes·taui, who was son of the king here indicated) are inserted to bring the 511 of Josephus into agreement with the xvi. 518 of his author Manetho ; some years are required for his campaigns against the Hyksos.   The insertion by Josephus of Armesses Miamun and of a duplicate

	Y. M.	B.C.
Dynasty xv.	259, 10	2199
Rest of Hyksos	251, 2	1939
Jacob's Eïsode		1896
Alisfragmouthosis	[7], 0	1688
Sum (stated 511)	518, 0	
xviii. 1-14 (Tethmosis—Armais)	246, 0	1681
[Sethos	60, 0]	
Ramesses i.	1, 4	1435
Armesses Miamun	66, 2	1374
Amenofis [Manetho's leper Exode]	19, 6	1308
Sum	393, 0	
Sethosis	59, 0	1288
Rampses ii.	66, 0	1229
Amenofis (=Merenptah) and Manetho's leper Exode according to Jos.	}	1163
Sum	518, 0	

Sethos are absolutely unauthorised ; they were put in to get his 393 years : which 393 is really the number of years from Aahmes to the 20th of Merenptah, 1580-1187. Why he went out of his way to forge this insertion is a mystery; his argument, such as it is, would have been just as good without it.   I can only guess that he had made up his mind to make Merenptah the Pharaoh of Manetho's leper Exode ;

and had he not duplicated the numbers of the two long reigns he would either have had to acknowledge that the former Amenofath or Amenofis was the Pharaoh in question (to which acknowledgment he was as averse as modern chronologers are), or else he would have had to leave him out altogether : a thing beyond the daring of any chronologer before the present century, although now it requires considerable courage to acknowledge his existence.

The minuter details concerning the 2 brothers have already been discussed under the dynasties. It remains to account for the transposition of Apofis and Apakhnan in Dyn. xv.

I have already shown that the order of xviii. has been disturbed by reading the kings *boustrofedon* ; the same explanation applies to

xv. 1 . 2 3 . 4 5 . 6	having been read as	1 . 2 4 . 3 5 . 6

This method of reading was used in all the extracts made by Josephus from Manetho (they extend only to Dyn. xv., xviii.), and as this kind of dislocation never occurs elsewhere, I attribute it to Josephus himself. Of course he was followed by the other post-Christian writers who preferred his authority to that of the native Egyptians. Unfortunately his influence in weightier matters has extended even to the present time.

8. AFRICANUS (ITEMS).

I will now give my reasons for not regarding the items of Africanus as an accurate representation of Manetho's scheme. The express statement of Synkellos, that Manetho reckoned one Sothic cycle down to 2024 B.C., *i.e.*, to the accession of Usertsen i., necessitates the adoption of the lowest numbers for i., iv., vi., and the omission of Amenemhat i. in the legitimate succession. In no other way can a total of 1461 years be obtained. Africanus' items for i.–vi. are therefore $10+7+6=23$ years in excess over Manetho's. But passing from this Memphite period to the Theban, we find in xviii., xix., xxi., xxii., a deficiency in Africanus of $1+4+16+2=23$ years, exactly counterbalancing this excess ; and in every instance the detailed examination of the dynasties shows that Africanus is in error. The clear inference is that he transferred these 23 years from after the expulsion of the Hyksos to before that time for some reason of his own. The following statement gives the reason :

Africanus' calculation is

Joseph before Pharoah	2017	in the 17th year of Apofis
Jacob's Eisode 9 years afterwards	2008	„ 26th „
Exodus 215 years after this	1797	in the first year of Khebron

In order to get the date 1797 he had not only to use the fictitious dynasty of 143 years introduced

by the Redactor, as I have already explained, but
also to omit 23 years which he preferred to scatter
over several dynasties rather than to subtract at
once from the Redactor's 143. This necessitated
the introduction of the 23 years in i.–vi. in order
not to disturb his grand total, which was doubtless
already calculated. He gets his data for Jacob
thus :

From 26th to 61st of Apofis	. . . .	39 years
Dyn. xvii. .	. . . . . .	151 ,,
Amosis .	. . . . . .	25 ,,
		215

These numbers are all taken without alteration
from Synkellos. There is a palpable error of 4
years in the dates 2017, 2008, which should read
2021, 2012, and this error is expressly noted by
Synkellos. It arose, doubtless, from Africanus
writing 2017 (when the 17th year of Apofis was
in his mind) instead of 2021 ; but it vitiates all
his artificial alterations to that extent. Now we
can see why he shifted the place of Apofis from
3 to 6 in Dyn. xv., and how the 24 years excess in
that dynasty was introduced by leaving 61 years
for Apakhnan in place of 37, and so necessitating
the reduction of 24 years in Dyn. xii. All this
confusion is undoubtedly due to Africanus.

Note that although he does include xvii. and xx.
in his calculation, he entirely omits xvi. He also
omits xiv. and xiii. For his dates are :

5500	Creation		2551	Dyn. xi.	43 years
2839	Peleg	339 years	2508	Amenemhat	16 ,,
2500			2492	xii.	160 ,,
			2232	xv.	284 ,,
			1948	xvii.	151 ,,
			1797	Exodus	

There is no room for xiii. or xiv. with their
453 + 184 = 637 years. He considers that there were
two parallel streams of kings—one Memphite, the
other Theban—each beginning in the time of Peleg;
but the Memphite somewhat earlier than the Theban.
It were too curious and profitless to look for exact
detail, but, taking a very rough approximation, this
was his view:

c. 2680. Menes.
   1870. Building the great pyramid under Kheops.
   1797. Exodus.

I have noted under Dyn. xviii. the confusion he
there introduced in o der to get rid of Amosis as
the first king.

As his numbers for i.–vi. come down to about
his epoch of Dyn. xx. it·is not probable that he
included vii.–x. in his legitimate kings. The only
dynasties of the 10 omitted in the Manethonic
reckoning which he did include were xi., xvii., xx.

THE MANETHONIC TOTALS.

I will now compare the totals as given in the
version of Africanus (from the Redactor) with those
of Eusebius. The statements in Africanus are as
follows:

Dyn.	i.–ii.	555 years	
	i.–iii.	769	
	i.–iv.	1046	
	i.–v.	1294	
	i.–vi.	1497	
	i.–viii.	1639, 70 d.	
	i.–xi.	2300, 70 d.	192 kings (and so Eusebius)

The details for all the first volume are as follows :

MANETHO'S VOL. I.

	YEARS.				KINGS.			
DYN.	AFR.	COR.	EUS.	COR.	AFR.	COR.	EUS.	COR.
i.	253		252		8		8	
ii.	302		297		9		9	
iii.	214		197		9		8	
iv.	274	277 ⎫	448	⎧ 300	8		17 ⎫	17
v.	248	⎭		⎩ 248	9		31 ⎭	
vi.	203		203		6		6	
	1494	1497	1397	1497	49	49	79	48
vii.	0, 70	4	75		70 ⎫		5	4
viii.	146		100		27 ⎬ 27		5	5
ix.	409	109	100		19 ⎭		4 ⎫	19
x.	185		185		19 ⎭		19 ⎭	
xi.	43	343	43	343	16	16	16	
Am. i.	16		—	—	1	1	1	—
	2293	2300	1900	2300	201	93	129	92

The total years in Africanus are deficient by 7, 3
of which are due to the reading 274 in iv. The true
number is 277, as shown by the totals 1046 for
i.–iv., &c. The total i.–viii. which requires 274
must be from a later hand than the others—prob-

ably the Redactor's.   The other 4 years must be inserted somewhere between vii. and x.   The only likely place is in vii., where it fits in with the numbers in Eratosthenes, as we have seen under the head of Dynasties.

The years in Eusebius show a deficiency of 400. Of these, 100 is almost certainly to be supplied in iv., v.   He reckoned, I suppose, 248 for v., and 300 for iv., including Kerferes' 26 years in iv. 1.   He ought, therefore, to have 18 kings for iv. and v., instead of which he has 17 and a most absurd 31. The text is clearly corrupt: this 31 cannot come from Eusebius' own hand.

Eusebius' 275 years for vii.–ix. are important. They show that there is an excess of 300 in Africanus ix., which I have transferred to xi., where they are absolutely necessary for the 16 kings, see- ing that the 6 or 7 kings of the Turin list have 243 years and the monuments testify to a large excess over 104.   The retention of this 43 years and rejection of 16 kings by modern chronologers cannot be defended. Moreover, Africanus' numbers for vii.–ix. when thus corrected give a total of 259, exactly 16 in deficit of Eusebius' 275, showing that Eus. reckoned the 16 of Amenemhat i. in his 75 for Dyn. vii., the right place for them, immediately after vi.   His total is there- fore a true Manethonic one; but the round centuries of which it is partly made up are probably guesses of his own; and the Africanus' sums are to be preferred.

The kings in Africanus are 9 in excess of the number stated, and may be reconciled by reading

10 for 19 in either ix. or x. The corruption of the kings, however, seems to be deeper than this. The generally correct numbers for the years imply a fairly accurate number of kings ; and I have shown under the Dynasties that we cannot assume more than about 27 for vii.-x. I would reject the 70 kings who reigned one day each as a late insertion : take the 27 of viii. as a total of vii.-x. written in mistake, and leave out the 19s as insertions of another minor total of ix. and x. The true reckoning I take to be vii., 4 kings; viii., 8 or 9 kings (according as Neferkara, who was probably contemporary with Dadkashemera, is omitted, as in Erastosthenes, or included, as in the Turin list) ; ix., 12 kings ; x., 7 kings ; in all 31 or 32 kings ; but if Amenemhat be counted in place of the contemporary 4 kings of vii., only 28 or 29 kings. The total number for the 1st vol. of Manetho is then 93, or, if Amenemhat be relegated to his proper place in Dyn. xii., 92 exactly; 100 less than the number stated.

For Eusebius I would in like manner take 19 as a total of ix.-x., and therefore omit his 4 kings in ix. ; and I would read 4 for 5 in Dyn. vii., which we know to be the true number, and so get the same total—92. Any less amount of correction than this will not reconcile the two lists, and, if 192 be retained as the true total, Eusebius' 129 is quite inexplicable.

MANETHO'S VOL. II.

	YEARS.				KINGS.			
DYN.	AFR.	COR.	EUS.	COR.	AFR.	COR.	EUS.	COR.
xii.	160	184	245	{ 16 { 184	7		7	
xiii.	453		453		60		60	
xiv.	184		484		76		76	
xv.	284	260	250		6		—	19
xvi.	518		190		32	15	5	8
xvii.	151		103		43	10	4	16
xviii.	263		348		16		14	16
xix.	209		194		6		5	6
Totals	2222	2222	2267	2222	246	196	171 +	196

Of the transposal of 24 years from xii. to xv.
enough has already been debated.   The total of
Eusebius imperatively demands the cancelling of the
45 years in xii. ; this also has been discussed.   As
Africanus and Eusebius, after these corrections,
agree, and it is not possible to alter any items in
this group that shall affect both of them by 101
years, it is clear that there is an error of that amount
in the total stated as 2121 years; it should read
2222.   But the extraordinary discrepancies between
Eusebius and Africanus require further explanation.
Eusebius is certainly wrong, as proved by the monuments.   He got his errors in this way.   He took his
dynasties xvi., xvii., xviii., xix. from the Chronicle
wrongly interpreted, and so got involved in a deficit
of 316 years: to correct this he added 300 to the
obscure xiv., and then transferred the 16 years of

Amenemhat i. to this volume as part of xii., and so got a perfect balance, and retained the sum of 2222 years.

As to the kings, xvi. and xvii. in Africanus are palpably absurd : the true numbers, as I have tried to show under the Dynasties, were probably 15 and 10 ; certainly not less than these. If we adopt these, the total becomes 196, just 100 more than is stated, compensating for the 100 overstated in vol. i. It is very tempting to reckon only xii., xiii., xv., xviii., xix. as 7, 60, 6, 16, 7 = 96, omitting xiv., xvi., xvii. as contemporary ; but, as the years of all the dynasties are added, this would not be admissible.

Eusebius, in his sum for xix., had certainly 6 kings (including Ramses iii.) ; and in xviii. he had 16 (including Amersis and Rathos) ; for xvi. he must have had 8 kings, from the Chronicler, whom he has followed exactly in the other 5 numbers. The missing number required for xv. (which is the xvii. of other authors) is 19 if his total was 196, 15 if 192 (he states it as 92). Synkellos (in the "Sothis book") has also 8 kings, not 5 ; and 190 years for "the xvi.th dynasty of Manetho," and he nearly always follows Eusebius, if anybody.

MANETHO'S THIRD VOLUME.

(See Table on next page.)

No totals are stated for the kings, and the 1050 for the years is given only in Africanus ; the necessary insertion of 191 years to get the total has already been fully discussed, and as no totals are given for Eusebius, any comparison becomes impossible. I have given the numbers, however, so as to make the table complete.

	YEARS.		KINGS.	
DYN.	AFR.	EUS.	AFR.	EUS.
xx.	135	172	12	12
xxa.	[143]	—	[4]	
xxi.	130	130	7	7
xxii.	120	49	9	3
	[48]	—	—	—
xxiii.	89	44	4	3
xxiv.	6	44	1	1
xxv.	40	44	3	3
xxvi.	150, 6	171	9	10
xxvii.	124, 4	120, 4	7	7
xxviii.	6, 0	6, 0	1	1
xxix.	20, 4	21, 4	4	4
xxx.	38, 0	20, 0	3	3
	1050, 2	821, 8	64	54

9. EUSEBIUS.

This author places the Exodus in 1511 B.C., the Eisode of Jacob in the 11th of Apofis, 1726 B.C. If the reigns of Amersis and Rathos are not restored as I have given them in Dyn. xviii., Joseph's standing before Pharaoh will not fall in the time of Apofis, as it must do in all these post-Christian schemes. The discrepancy between the items and the sum stated in this instance is therefore due to a scribe's omission of the reigns, and not to a different reckoning, as in the sums and items of Africanus. Note, however,

that he has not succeeded in getting the true year
of Apofis ; in fact, he could not, as his Apofis has no
17th year, his reign being reduced to 14 instead of
61, in order to get his dynasty xvii. within the
Procrustean limit fixed by his adoption of the
Chronicle numbers.

There are other instances of discrepancy between
the sums and items :

	SUM.	ITEMS.		SUM.	ITEMS.
i.	252	228	xix.	194	162
xii.	245	182	xxii.	44	49
xviii.	348	317	xxvi.	167	171

In i. the sum 252 is undoubtedly the true reading,
and the items must be corrected, reading, perhaps,
54 for Menes, or 34 for Menes and 47 for Athotis.
In xii. the 182 is certainly from another version, but
with the 16 years added for Ammenemes, it differs
only by 2 years from the 200, to which I have
already shown that the 245 must be reduced. In
xviii. the sum is right, as we have just seen.   In
xix. 32 years have been deducted for Ramses iii., and
37 added to Dyn. xx., thus getting $194 - 32 = 162$,
as in the items of xix. and $135 + 37 = 172$ for xx.
In xxii. the true number is certainly xlix., not xliv.,
as shown by the corresponding items in Africanus.
Finally, in xxvi., Vafres should probably have 19
years and Nekhao 8, as in Africanus, so that the sum
would again be correct.

Eusebius reckoned xiii.–xvi. (including his xv.,
the xvii. of Africanus) as contemporary kings thus :

5199	Creation				
2559	Peleg				
2220			2369	Dyn. xi.	343 years
			2026	xii.	200
			1826	xvii.	103
			1723	xviii. 1–4	212
			1511	Exodus	

If we were to include 250 years for xv., and leave out my conjectural years in xi., Peleg's dates would be equally well satisfied; but then the totals would require a reading of ix. 400 years, which is quite inconsistent with the " 4 kings." I have put the 300 years in the only possible place.

Like Africanus, Eusebius held that there were two series—one of Memphite, one of Theban kings; his Memphites (very roughly) come thus:

c. 2500. Menes.
1720. Great pyramid; while the Hebrews were in Egypt and in the time of Joseph!

10. THE SOTHIS BOOK.

Finally, we arrive at the list of the 86 Mestræan kings given by Synkellos with definite dates. These have never been sufficiently considered. It is true that for the dynasties given in full by Manetho they are inaccurate, imperfect, and have been manipulated in the most extravagant manner, very often following blindly the blind guidance of Eusebius. But for certain dynasties, xi., xvii., xix., xx., xxα. it has certainly followed some authority unknown to us, and is of considerable value. It has also been found of use for Dyn. xv., xxvi. Synkellos reckons Creation, 5500 B.C.; Peleg, 2729–2490; Joseph's death, 1827; the Exodus, 1684. I give here his list in full, with his notes on certain kings.

Dyn.	No.	Kings.	Years.	Sums.	B.C.
xi. 4	1	Mestraim (Mĕnĕs)	35		2724
5	2	Kourŏdĕs	63		2689
6	3	Aristarkos	34		2626
7	4	Spanios	36		2592
8	5		72		2556
9	6	}		240	
xii. 1	7	Serapis	23		2484
2	8	Sesonkhosis	49		2461
3	9	Amenemes	29		2412
5	10	Amasis	2		2383
6	11	Akesefthres	13		2381
7	12	Ankhozeus	9		2368
8	13	Armiyses	4	129	2359
xvii. 2	14	Khamois	12		2355
3	15	Miamous	14		2343
4	16	Amesesis	65		2329
5	17	Ouses	50	141	2264
xvi. 1	18	Rameses	29		2214
2	19	Ramessomencs	15		2185
3	20	Ousimares	31		2170
4	21	Ramesseseos	23		2139
5	*22	Ramessameno	19		2116
6	23	Ramesse Ioubasse	39		2097
7	24	Ramesse Ouafrou	29		2058
8	*25	Konkharis	5	190	2029
xv. 1	26	Silites	19		2024
2	27	Baion	44		2005
3	28	Apakhnas	36		1961
4	*29	Afofis	61		1925
5	30	Sethos	50		1864
6	31	Kertos (44y. Man.)	29		1814
7	*32	Aseth	20	259	1785
xviii. 1	33	Amosis (Tethmosis)	26		1765
2	34	Khebron	13		1739
3	35	Amemfes	15		1726
4	36	Amenses	11		1711
5	37	Misfragmouthosis	16		1700
6	38	Misfres	23		1684
7	39	Touthmosis	39		1661
8	*40	Amenofthis	34		1622
9	41	Oros	48		1588
10	42	Akhenkheres	25		1540

Dyn.	No.	Kings.	Years.	Sums.	B.C.
xviii. 11	43	Athoris	29		1515
12	44	Khenkheres	26		1486
13	45	Akherres (? 30)	8		1460
14	*46	Armaios (Danaos)	9	323	1452
xix. 2	47	Ramesses (Aigyptos)	68	(? 345)	1443
3	48	Amenofis	8		1375
5a	49	Thouoris	17		1367
5	50	Nekhepsos	19	112	1350
xx. 1-3	51	Psammouthis	13		1331
4-5	52		4		1318
6-7	53	Kertos (16 yrs.)	[20]		1314
8-9	54	Rampsis	45	82	1294
xix. 4a	55	Amenses (Ammenemes)	26		1249
4	56	Okhyras	14	40+112	1223
xxi. 1	57	Amendes	27		1209
2	*58	Thouoris	50	77	1182
xxa. 1	*59	Athothis (Fousanos)	28		1132
2	60	Kenkenes	39		1104
3	61	Ouennefes	42		1065
4	*62	Sousakeim	34	143	1023
xxi. 7	63	Psouenos	25		989
4	64	Ammenofis	9		964
3	65	Nefekheres	6		955
5	66	Saites	15		949
6	67	Psinakhes	9	64+77	934
xxiii. 1	68	Petoubastes	44		925
2	69	Osorthon	9		881
3	70	Psammos	10	63	872
xxii. 1	71	Konkaris	21		862
2	72	Osorthon	15		841
6	73	Takelofis	13	49	826
xxiv. 1	*74	Bokkhoris	44	44	813
xxv. 1	*75	Sabakon	12		769
2	76	Sebekhon	12		757
3	77	Tarakes	20	44	745

Dyn.	No.	Kings.	Years.	Sums.	B.C.
xxvi. 1	78	Amaes	38		725
2	79	Stefinathes	27		687
3	80	Nekhepsos	13		660
4	81	Nekhao	8		647
5	82	Psammetikhos	14		639
6	83	Nekhao ii.	9		625
7	84	Psammouthis (Psammetikhos)	17		616
8	85	Ouafris	34		599
9	86	Amosis	50	210	565
					515

Notes.—22. "In the time of this king [2114 B.C.] Abraham went down into Egypt."

25. "700 years of 25 kings of the cycle in Manetho called Cynic end with the 5th year of this king" [2024 B.C.].

29. "Some say that in the 4th year of his reign [1921 B.C.] Joseph ame into Egypt as a slave; he established Joseph lord of Egypt and of all his kingdom in the 17th year of his reign" [1906 B.C.], &c.

32. "This king added the 5 Epagomenæ, and in his time they say the Egyptian year was reckoned as 365 days, having before his time counted only 360. In his time the heifer was made a god and called Apis."

40. "This is Memnon, &c.," as in Africanus and Eusebius. "Ethiopians from the river Indus settled in Egypt."

46. The story of the brothers Danaos and Aigyptos is given here much as in Josephus. Danaos is called Armaios (Horemhib); but Aigyptos (the Amenofath of Manetho, the Amenofis of Josephus), is confused with Ramessu ii., and Ramessu i. and Seti i. are altogether omitted.

58. "This is the Polybus husband [son] of Alexandra, celebrated by Homer in the Odyssey [iv. 126]," &c. But 49 is certainly the Polybus of Manetho.

59. "In his time earthquakes took place through Egypt; they had not happened there before."

62. "Sousakeim took prisoners before Jerusalem: Libyans, Ethiopians, Treglodytes."

74, 75. Same notices as in Manetho.

GENEALOGIES.

The genealogies of priests and others are, when obtainable in sufficient numbers, admirable supple-

ments to other data and have been made use of by
Brugsch, &c., from Dynasty xxi. to Dynasty xxvi. His
application of the same principle to the earlier times
fails ; not because the principle is wrong, but because
sufficient data are wanting for the application.   His
doctrine that reigns may be taken as generations is
not sound : in fact, an average reign is only two-
thirds of an average generation.

As to later or minor authorities, Diodorus, &c., I
shall scarcely ever have to notice them, and certainly
need not in this place.   One name, however, Castor
(c. 150 B.C.) I must specially mention as serviceable
(though only indirectly) in the matter of artificial
chronology, not for historic purposes ; but he throws
light on the methods in vogue among ancient chronologers, and, moreover, has never to my knowledge
been correctly edited.

Castor's reckoning from Excerptor Barbaro-latinus ap. Scalig.

Gods.	Years.	
Hephæstus	680	
Sol Hephæsti fil.	77	
[Agatho-dæmon and Cronus]		
Osinosiris	420	
Orus Stoliarchus	28	
Typhon	45	
Demigods.		
Anubis	83	
Apion [Hercules]	77	
[6 Demigods	140]	
Colliguntur Deorum regna		1550
Ecynii [P I E Cynici]		2100
		3650

Hæc finis de primo tomo Manethonis habens annos 2100.

CASTOR.	KINGS.	YEARS.	AFRICANUS.	
i. Mineus [Menes] and 7 descendants	8	253	8	253
ii. [Boethus and] 8 others	9	302	9	302
iii. Necherocheus [Necherophes] and 8 others	9	214	9	214
iv. [Soris and] 17 others	18	214	8	274
[error		3		3]
v. [Userkheres and] 21 others	22	258	9	248
vi. Othoes and 7 others	8	203	6	203
viii. 14 others	14	140	27	146
[error				4]
ix. 20 others	20	409	19	409
(x.), xi. 7 others	7	204	35	244
Totals	115	2200	130	2300

CASTOR.	YEARS.	AFRICANUS.	YEARS.
xii. Diospolites	[15]9	Diospolites	160
xiii. Bubastites	153	Diospolites	453
xiv. Tanites	184	Xoites	184
xv. Sebennites	224	Shepherds	284
xvi. Memphites	318	Shepherds	518
xvii. Heliopolites	221	Shepherds and Thebans	151
xviii. Hermopolites	26[1]	Diospolites	263
Totals	1520		2013

Usque ad 17ᵐᵃᵐ· [he omits vii., x.] potestatem scribitur tomus habens 1520 annos.

The numbers of the dynasties (i., ii., &c.) are inserted by me; there are none in the original.

The scheme ends at the end of Dynasty xviii., that is, at the epoch of Menofres (Ramses i. 1318 B.C.), the beginning of a new Sothic period. As the Sothic

period of Castor ends at the close of Dynasty xi.
he probably meant the 1520 years of Manetho's
vol. ii. to run contemporaneously with the last 1520
years of his vol. i.

In this reckoning Osinosiris evidently includes the
3 gods Shu, Seb and Asar, the 420 years being 3×140;
and 6 demigods with 140 years have dropped out as
shown by the total 1550 : restoring those we have 7
gods, 8 demigods, and 115 kings [PIE] of the Cynic
cycle with years $2100 = 15 \times 140$: 130 kings in all,
and 3650 years or $2\frac{1}{2}$ Sothic periods (compare the
mythical Dynasty iii. of the Memphite school, which
has 30 demigods and 3650 years).   In its present
form this scheme must date after the time when the
Sothic reckoning was established.   But there was an
earlier scheme ; Suidas under Hefaistos gives him
1680 years $= 12 \times 140$, and this would make the total
4650 years $= 155 \times 30$ or 155 Seds, the demigods
having 300 or 10 Seds ; the gods 2250 or 75 Seds ;
and the Cynic cycle 2100 or 70 Seds.   The original
calculation was certainly by Seds, and the change to
a Sothic total shows that we have here a genuine
tradition of the mythic numbers and no mere inven-
tion of Castor's.   The occurrence of the factor 140 in
no less than four places shows that this number also
had some special significance, perhaps 5 Seds of 28
years or 2 Precessional degrees of 70 ; but this is
beside my present purpose.

Passing to Manetho's first volume the total must
read 2100 not 2200 ; the error lies probably in
Dyn. xi. which should read 104 years : the omission
of 3 years in Dynasty iv. is accounted for by the

parallel omission of 3 years in Manetho which I have noted before; but Castor's object being evidently to diminish Manetho's total by exactly 200 years he has left all the unit figures unchanged : this shows that he corrected the outstanding error of 4 years in Manetho by adding 4 years to Dynasty viii. not to vii. as I have done. The entire omission of Dynasty vii. is especially noteworthy.

In the number of kings 17 in iv. has probably arisen from adding in the 9 kings of v. $(8 + 9 = 17)$; Eusebius has copied this error; the 21 in v. is entirely wrong, but Eusebius here improves on him and has 31; 8 in vi. and 14 in viii. are genuine corrections, but the following 7 is quite erroneous.

For Manetho's second volume it is clear that we must insert 150 years in Dynasty xii. and 1 year in xviii. : there is the same vacillation of one year in Manetho in this latter dynasty. The total is thus brought into agreement with the items. The names of the dynasties are also noticeable, especially his calling the Shepherds of xvi. Memphites from their seat of government at Memphis, and the Diospolite worshippers of Tahuti (Hermes), the Tahutmes' and Aahmes of xviii., Hermopolites.

NOTE ON THE SUPPOSED ANTIQUITY OF BABYLONIA.

There is an inscription of Nabonidos to the effect that Kudur Turgu or Kudur Bau, father of Sagarakti Burgas, lived 800 years before his time, 556 B.C. But neither after Nazri Maruttas, where Sayce places these kings, nor after Kallima Sin, where Hilprecht locates them, will the known facts admit them to be inserted.   If for "8 hundreds" we read "8 sosses" the 800 years is reduced to 480 and the date of Kudur Turgu becomes 1036 B.C.   He and his son would then be the two missing Elamites of Dyn. vii.   I have little doubt this is a true conjecture.

In like manner the inscription of Nabonidos (dating near the end of his reign) which says "The foundation cylinder of Naram Sin, son of Sargon, which for 3200 years no king who had gone before had seen, Samas . . . showed unto me," should read "3 neri and 2 sosses" (1920) instead of "3 thousands and 2 hundreds." Naram Sin's date would then be 2470 B.C. instead of 3750 as usually assumed.

On this one cylinder (as I believe wrongly interpreted) rests the stupendous chronology at present universally advocated by the Assyriologists.

SECTION V.

CONCLUSIONS.

I WILL now state the final results that appear to me to be warranted by the evidence adduced.

1. The only two ancient schemes that have reached us which state a complete total for the whole period from Menes to Okhos, that is to say, the Chronicle and the Redactor, although widely differing in amount, agree in this : that neither of them allows of more

than 20 successive dynasties, the others being regarded as contemporary. Nor can I discover any evidence that any ancient authority took a different view from theirs. The monuments on detailed examination appear to confirm their opinion. I therefore adopt the legitimate succession as indicated by Manetho (in his omission of detailed reigns for Dyn. vii.–xi. ; xiii.–xiv.; xvi.–xvii. ; xx.) as including only Dyn. i.–vi. ; xii: xv.; xviii.–xix. ; xxi.–xxx.

2. There were among the ancients two schools of chronology (as there are now), one advocating a short, the other a long system : the differences between these are confined to Dyn. i.–vi. and Dyn. xii., xv. For the second of these periods the long Manethonic system is almost certainly right : for the first it is certainly wrong. The excess in Dyn. i.–vi. is made up of supposititious reigns (Sesokhris, Mesokhris, Soyfis, Akhes, &c.), exaggerated regnal years (Soufis, Menkheres, &c.), and reckonings of co-regnant kings as if they were independent and sole (Rhatoises, Bikheris, &c.). In no one instance has any statement of regnal years in the Turin papyrus been proved to conflict with the monuments ; in many (such as the career of Raskhemka) the Manethonic numbers are impossible. I therefore reject Manetho as an authority for Dyn. i.–vi. ; I shall presently state how and why I accept him for xii., xv. From this point onwards the short and long schemes virtually coincide.

3. I have reserved for this place a hypothesis with regard to the short schemes which will, I trust, explain their construction and obviate all outstanding

difficulties in the way of rejecting the longer one for
Dyn. i.–vi. I have desired to keep the body of the
work free from conjecture as far as possible : but
here the contradictions are so palpable that some
hypothesis is absolutely necessary. Taking the
Turin papyrus as our starting-point, Dyn. iii., iv., vi.
present no difficulty, but the other dynasties, i.–ii., v.,
vii.–x. (the contemporary equivalent for xii., xv.) each
show a deficiency. For vii.–x. it gives only 355
years against Manetho's 444, which are confirmed by
every detail on careful examination—89 years
deficient ; for v. it has only 66 years against 190 in
the Chronicle, which is certainly right as shown on
comparison with Manetho's details—deficit 124 years;
and for i., ii. there is again a deficit probable of not
more than 52 years, as shown by comparison with
Manetho's numbers, which judging from all the
parallel instances where direct comparison is possible
are almost certain to be in excess : I take the deficit
at 26 years, half of 52. It will not do to assume
that any of these deficiencies can be supplied from
the destroyed parts of the papyrus ; this is precluded
by the total of 755 years at the end of Dyn. vi.
Hereon I ground my hypothesis.

The only epochs anterior to Ramessu ii. (when we
know the Turin list to have been formed and the
Abydos tablet to have been erected) at which chronological schemes are likely to have been made are in
the reigns of Thotmes iii., when the chamber of
ancestors was sculptured, and of Ramessu i., the Sed
epoch of Menofres. Taking this epoch, 1318 B.C., for
starting-point, 89 years will lead us to 1229, the

45th year of Ramessu ii. in the one direction, and
$124 + 26 = 150$ in the other lands us in 1468, the
36th of Thotmes iii., this last being, of course, liable
to future correction of a few years either way. I
assume, then, that the original calculation, which is
the nearest approximation to the truth at present
obtainable, was made for Thotmes iii. ; that when it
was revised for Ramessu i. the excision was made of
26 years in Dyn. i., ii. and 124 years in Dyn. v. ; and
again, when our extant Turin list was drawn up for
Ramessu ii. a further excision of 89 years (out of the
hated Hyksos rule) was added to the former, thus
making the epochs of each of the 3 schemes exactly
1 Sothic cycle before the date at which each scheme
was made. This gives the following hypothetical
system :

Epochs.	First Scheme, T. 1.		Second. T. 2.		Third. T. P.	
	Years.	B.C.	Years.	B.C.	Years.	B.C.
i. Menes	905	2929	755	2779	755	2690
xii. Usertsen i.	184	2024	184	2024	184)	1935
xv. Khyan	260	1840	260	1840	171)	1751
xviii. Aahmes	20	1580	262	1580	262	1580
20 Aahmes	92	1560				
36 Tahutimes iii.		1468				
1 Ramessu i.				1318	89	1318
45 Ramessu ii.						1229

The only doubtful number in T. 1 is the 905 years,
which can only be 26 years in error at most; the
numbers in T. P. are fixed by the Turin list and
Mahler's calculation; but those in T. 2 remind us

so strongly of the Manethonic (Memphitic) divine dynasties as to make it worth while to examine what changes in them would be needed to bring them into agreement with my theory that these god-reigns are only history in disguise. Premising that the Ptah worship must be taken, as already pointed out, to begin in the 5th year of Menes, the following will give the divine dynasties (abridged) for the 3 schemes:

		T. 1.		T. 2.		T. P.	
DYN.	GODS.	YEARS.	B.C.	YEARS.	B.C.	YEARS.	B.C.
i.	Ptah	900	2924	750	2774	750	2684
xii.	Ra, &c.	184	2024	184	2024	183	1934
xv.	Asar, &c.	146	1840	146	1840	146	1751
	Harsiesis	25		25		25	
	Min to Sebek	89		89		—	
xviii.	Amen	20	1580	20	1580	20	1580
	Khons, &c.	92					
	Sum	1456	1468	1214		1124	

The numbers in T. 2 are taken unaltered from the Memphite scheme. I need only note that Manetho, who adopts them, gives a set of numbers for his men kings, which cannot be explained as in any way connected with the items of the divine dynasties; and yet it is hardly to be supposed that the coincidences of the B.C. dates 2024, 1840, 1580 with the epochs of xii., xv., xviii. is accidental. He must have got his numbers from one of the early forms of the Turin list. In T. 1 the only number changed is 900 years for Ptah instead of 9000 months as in T. 2, T. P., but without some such form of the list as

T. 1 no historical reason is evident for making an epoch at 1468 B.C. at the end of the "4 other demigods"; if this be not an epoch, the historic explanation, with its remarkable coincidences just noticed, would have to be thrown over. If it be admitted, 2929 must be the epoch of Menes. For T. P. we have a rough but ready test. The sum of the great gods and the followers of Harsiesis must be 13,420 (months) + less than 80 for the torn off tens and units: now 1124 years × 12 = 13,488, which fulfils this condition. The only change in T. P. is the omission of 3 demigods, the sum of whose years is 89, exactly the deficit of regnal years in the Turin papyrus, and whose position corresponds with that of the Hyksos kings in the history, another remarkable coincidence inexplicable except on the hypothesis now advocated. I can now leave this dubious hypothesis and give my view of the affiliation of all the ancient schemes.

MADE B.C.	UNDER	SCHEME.			
1468	Tahutimes iii.			T. 1	
1318	Ramessu i.			T. 2	
1229	Ramessu ii.			T. P.	Abydos
1204	Merenptah		(? 1 Chron.)		
1140	Ramessu iii.	(? 1 Erat.)			
571	Aahmes				Herod.
340	Okhos		2 Chron.		
287	Ptolemy ii.				Manetho
246	Ptolemy iii.	2 Erat.			
222	Ptolemy iv.				Redactor
					Afr. Eus. &c.

I have inserted 2 schemes, 1 Chronicle and 1 Eratosthenes, which may have served as bases of those which have come down to us; but these are purely hypothetical and may be omitted without affecting my argument, which is entirely independent of them. The rest of the table tells its own story.

4. The various systems of Sed festivals, as now set forth, and which must have been in use in at least 3 forms, as shown by the falling of the Sed days on Epifi 27, 28, and 30, are mainly useful in confirming dates reached by other lines of investigation. The exact agreement of the results in every case is most remarkable, and it cannot be obtained on any hypothesis that refuses the contemporaneity of the 10 dynasties rejected by the ancient authorities from legitimate succession. As, however, most of these were of late introduction, and only used calculated, not observed, dates, they are of little use for Dyn. i.-vi. : the exceptional system is that of the Tybi epoch, which was certainly in actual use as early as 2751 (or possibly 2781 B.C.), the epoch of its origin. This date 2751 falls in the reign of Kakau, to whom the Manethonic tradition attributes a religious innovation—namely, the deification of the sacred bulls. I have little doubt that the hieratic system, including the institution of these festivals, was organised in his time. This leaves only Dyn. i. or ii. as of doubtful duration, and the variant readings for Menes' reign (62 or 30 years) more than cover the 26 years that are possibly doubtful. The epoch of Menes cannot be far from 2929 B.C. The Sed systems may be thus tabulated :

Established B.C.	Epoch.	
2751 Kakau	1 Tybi	2751
1631 Staan	1 Thoth	2779
1468 Tahutimes iii.	1 Famenoth	2059 ⎫
571 Aahmes	1 Famenoth	2031 ⎭
243	1 Pakhons	

5. I have no space even to enumerate fully the anomalies and difficulties removed by the system now proposed : such as the abolition of huge gaps of many centuries, during which the monuments are absolutely silent; the extinction of incredible hypotheses as to the oscillation of Egyptian art from an ideal perfection to imbecility and *vice versâ;* as to sudden abnegation of pyramid building for centuries during Dyn. vii.-x. and as sudden resumption thereof, and the like ; the explanation of the numbers in Herodotus, and the vindication of the grand old traveller's accuracy ; the exact agreement with the chronology of the Babylonians and the Hebrews (which is, however, rather indicated than proved in the present essay); the satisfaction of all subsidiary tests, such as the Ramessean inscription in the 400th year of Setaanubti : all such will be evident to the careful reader. But I may draw attention to the fact that there are in this book several distinct lines of investigation, which may be by the reader, and have been by the author, examined independently— viz., the evidences of the numerical schemes, the formation of divine dynasties, the observation of Sed festivals, and the artificial use of Sothic and other cycles : the conclusions obtained from all and each of

these, with only the introduction of a single unauthorised number, have been shown to be consistent; and if this consensus is accidental the doctrine of chances may be given up at once, and historical investigation banished from the realm of science. I have no doubt that many petty details may have to be amended, but the main theses of this essay—the contemporaneity of the 10 illegitimate dynasties, and the exaggerations of Manetho in Dyn. i.-vi.—cannot be henceforth evaded as they are in the received systems of modern chronologers.

I. DATA.

	SHORT CHRONOLOGY.			LONG CHRONOLOGY.			
DYN.	TURIN.	CHRON.	ERAT.	MAN.	RED.	AFR.	EUS.
D.G.				214	214		
i.	⎫ 508	443	⎧ 190	253	253	263	252
ii.	⎪		⎪ 161	302	302	302	297
iii.	⎬		⎨ 53	214	214	214	197
iv.	⎪		⎪ 97	277	274	284	[5]48
v.	66	190	68	218	248	218	
vi.	⎱ 181	103	107	197	203	203	203
vii.	⎰	736	⎧ 22	(14)	—	[4]	75
viii.	755	348	⎨ 38	(146)	—	146	100
ix.	⎱ 355		⎪ 129	(109)	—	[4]09	100
x.	⎰		⎩ 185	(185)	—	185	185
	1110	1084	SOTH.				
xi.	(243)	—	240	[3]43	16	[3]43	[3]43
xii.	(213)	—	129	184	184	160	[200]
xiii.	?	—	—	(453)	—	453	453
xiv.	?	—	—	(184)	—	184	484
xv.	?	—	259	260	260	284	250
xvi.		—	190	(518)	—	518	190
xvii.		⎰ 194 ⎱	141	(151)	—	151	103
xviii.		⎱ [50] ⎰	323	⎧ 263	263	262	348
xix.		228	152	⎨ 209	209	204	194
xx.		—	82	(135)	—	135	172
xxa.		—	143	—	[143]	(143)	—
xxi.		[128] ⎱	141	⎧ 130	130	114	130
xxii.		⎰ 121 ⎱	49	⎨ 166	120	116	49
		⎱ 48 ⎰			[48]		
xxiii.		19 ⎱	63	⎧ 89	89	89	44
xxiv.		44 ⎪	44	⎪ 6	6	6	44
xxv.		44 ⎬	44	⎨ 40		40	44
xxvi.		177 ⎰	210	⎩ 150, 6	150, 6	151	171
xxvii.		124	ERAT.	120, 4	124, 4	124	120, 4
xxviii.		[6]	Total	6	6	6	6
xxix.		39 ⎱	1045	⎰ 20, 4	20, 4	20	21, 4
xxx.		18 ⎰	then	⎱ 38	38	38	20
			53 kings				
xxxi.	Totals	2324		3355, 6	3555	15	16

The numbers in loops of contemporary kings are omitted in the Manetho total.

II. RESULTS.

Dyn.	B.C.	Dyn.	B.C.	Dyn.	B.C.	Dyn.	B.C.
		i.	2929				
		ii.	2768				
		iii.	2553				
		iv.	2500				
xi. *a*	2381	v.	2396				
xi. *b*	2281	vi.	2205				
				xii. 1	2053		
xiii.	2038	vii.	2024	xii. 2	2024	xiv.	2024
		ix.	1874				
—	—	x.	1765	end	1840	xv., xvi.	1840
				xvii.	1731		
end	1585	end	1580	xviii.	1580	xvi.	1580
				xix.	1317	end	1322
xxi.	1108	xxii.	980	xx.	1108		
				end	973		

COTEMPORARY DYN. FROM CHRONICLE.

Dyn.	B.C.	Dyn.	B.C.				
xxiii.	812	xxiv.	728	23	811	24	792
xxv.	717	xxvi.	667	25	748	26	704
xxvii.	525	xxviii.	403	—	—	—	—
xxix.	398	xxx.	878	29	397	30	358
		end	340	—	—	end	340

L

TABLE I.—DATA.   TABLE II.—RESULTS.

In Table I. I give the years assigned to each of the xxx. Dynasties by the following authorities— for the short chronology: (1) The Turin papyrus. (2) The Old Chronicle. (3*a*) Eratosthenes i.-x. (3*b*) The list in Synkellos xi.-xxvi., sometimes called the Book of the Sothis, sometimes the Mestræan list, sometimes the traditional numbers, but usually referred to in the present work simply as "Synkellos." For the long chronology: (4) The original Manethonic numbers as deduced in the body of the essay. (5) The numbers of the Redactor's corruption as given in the actual sums stated in Africanus. (6) Africanus' own reckoning as given in his items. (7) Eusebius' reckoning.

The numbers inserted in brackets in columns 2, 5 are necessitated by the totals of the Chronicle and of the 3 Manethonic volumes, so that this one page (reserving col. 4, in which the arrangement is slightly conjectural) consists of all the various sums of dynastic numbers that have been handed down in any ancient scheme that has reached us; it is truly the table of data. (N.B.—All through the book the summation of the items of any one dynasty is called a "sum": that of several "sums" is called a "total." This saves much circumlocution.)

The numbers in brackets in cols. 6, 7 are conjectural; and so *passim*.

In Table II. I tabulate the ultimate results of my investigation. The dynasties enclosed in the thick lines are the legitimate or supreme dynasties of Manetho ; the others are subordinate and contemporary.   Only in Dyn. i.–vi. do I reject the Manethonic numbers and adopt those of the short chronology— iii., iv., vi. from the Turin list, v. from the Chronicle.

I have given the Chronicler's reckoning of the later dynasties in the lower right-hand corner.

The dates in the first column may be 2383, 2283, 2040, 1587, and in the second 1767, 1587.   I cannot find definite evidence on this small difference.   In the present state of our knowledge of the dynasties concerned, this is of absolutely no importance.

By introducing a white line here and there, this table has been made to indicate (roughly) to the eye the lapse of time from Menes on to Okhos ; each line represents one century.

ADDENDUM

THE attentive reader will note a discrepancy between the date given in the preface 2924 B.C. and that of 2929 B.C. with which I begin my tables : the explanation is this. While this book has been passing through the press I have been endeavouring to solve two problems : (1) Why the divine dynasties, supposing them to be founded on history (see p. 94, &c.), should have been exaggerated irregularly, some demigods' years being taken from the "month" numbers, and others from the "seasons"; (2) whether there is any trace in the schemes of a reckoning of the precession of the equinoxes, and, if so, to what amount. I cannot suppose, as some recent writers do, that the Egyptians of 2900–340 B.C. were acquainted with its true amount, $50''\!\cdot\!18$ in one year, or $1°$ in 71y. 9m. : the fact that Hipparchus (160–145 B.C.) could only state as limits $59''$ to $36''$ for the annual amount (or 61 to 100 years for $1°$ of precession) is sufficient to disprove this. But they may have reckoned much nearer to 71 or 72 years than the Chaldees, who seen to have taken 100 years. Now consider these numbers

Gods.	Years.		
Ptah	5400	= 75.	72
Aries entered	+3600	= 75.	48
Ra to Set	3000	= 75.	40
Har	300	= 75.	4
Anhur to Amen	1200	= 75.	16
Sum	13500	= 75.	180
4 others	370	= 74.	5
30 demigods	3650	= 73.	50
Total	17520	= 73.	240

The epochs of Ptah, Ra, and Har are just the most
likely to be distinguished in such a calculation, and
the interpretation I would suggest is that when the
Memphite numbers for the divine dynasties were
compiled as far as Amen, 180° of precession were
supposed to have been gone through before any
man king; of which 120° were assigned to Ptah; and
so forth. Then after many observations the priests
found that 75 years was too long an estimate and tried
74, which for the same reason was abandoned in favour
of 73. The final reduction (under Amosis xxvi. 8
I believe) has a total of 240° of 73 years each—*i.e.*,
of two-thirds of the whole precessional cycle : and it
is difficult to believe that this can be anything else
than a device of the priests to retain all the numerals
of the older calculation for 180,° half a precession
cycle, while correcting the time of 1° precession
for 75 years to 73. The older scheme may date
from Ramessu i. or Ramessu ii. The Egyptian
approximation of 73 years when the Chaldeans got

no nearer than 100 is very creditable. If this be so the conjectural 905 years in p. 154 should be reduced to $900 = 12 \times 75$, as an exact multiple of 75 is required, and for the first date in Dyn. i. we must read 2924 B.C. (Mena 30 years, as Eratosthenes has it) and the "single unauthorised number" of p. 159 will disappear.

I have not in the body of the work entered on the question of the kind of year in use at various times because I cannot adduce convincing evidence: however, to avoid the appearance of having neglected the question, I give here a statement of my belief, reserving all discussion for a future opportunity.

| | | | DAYS IN | | |
B.C.	DYNASTIES.		SACRED YEAR.	CIVIL YEAR.	SUPREME GOD.
2924	i.-vi.	Memphite	360	360	Ptah
2024	xii.	Theban	360	365	Ra
1840	xv.	Hyksos	364	365	Osiris
1749	Eisode	,,	365	365	Haroeris
1630	Staan	,,	365¼	365	Thoth

I also believe that the Egyptian deluge (the passage of the equinoctial point from Taurus to Aries) was reckoned by the Memphites at B.C. 2324; by the Thebans 2384; by the Babylonians 2334: but I cannot discuss this till I treat of Babylonian chronology.

In the table for the Memphite Divine Dynasties I have followed authority in making Horos = the

son of Isis, and Apollo = the son of Seb : I have
little doubt that these should be transposed and
that Plutarch was right in making the son of
Isis = Apollo.

Printed by BALLANTYNE, HANSON & Co.
London & Edinburgh

www.ingramcontent.com/pod-product-compliance
Lightning Source LLC
Chambersburg PA
CBHW030132030726

47498CB00007B/2664